P9-DGL-990

THE LIBRARY OF CONTEMPORARY THOUGHT

*America's most original voices
tackle today's most provocative issues*

SEYMOUR M. HERSH

AGAINST ALL ENEMIES
*Gulf War Syndrome:
The War Between America's Ailing
Veterans and Their Government*

"Kimo S. Hollingsworth of Shepherdstown, West Virginia, was deployed to the Gulf as a marine lieutenant in September 1991 and served as a platoon commander during the liberation of Kuwait. . . .

" 'As an American who volunteered to serve my country,' Hollingsworth told the committee, 'I can accept bad medical news. What I cannot accept and will not tolerate are professional bureaucrats that first deny a problem exists, then minimize problems once they surface, and lastly make the problems seem more complex so endless studies can be conducted. . . . The Department of Defense must learn that young men and women of this country are a valuable resource. I am a combat veteran, not an expendable item.' "

Also by Seymour M. Hersh

Chemical and Biological Warfare: America's Hidden Arsenal
My Lai 4: A Report on the Massacre and Its Aftermath
Cover-up: The Army's Secret Investigation
  of the Massacre of My Lai
The Price of Power: Kissinger in the Nixon White House
The Target Is Destroyed: What Really Happened to
  Flight 007 and What America Knew About It
The Samson Option: Israel's Nuclear Arsenal
  and America's Foreign Policy
The Dark Side of Camelot

AGAINST ALL ENEMIES

Gulf War Syndrome:
The War Between America's Ailing
Veterans and Their Government

SEYMOUR M. HERSH

THE LIBRARY OF CONTEMPORARY THOUGHT
THE BALLANTINE PUBLISHING GROUP • NEW YORK

The Library of Contemporary Thought
Published by The Ballantine Publishing Group

Copyright © 1998 by Seymour M. Hersh

http://www.randomhouse.com

Library of Congress Cataloging-in-Publication Data
Hersh, Seymour M.
Against all enemies : Gulf War syndrome, the war
between America's ailing veterans and their government /
Seymour M. Hersh.—1st ed.
p.   cm.
ISBN 0-345-42748-3 (alk. paper)
1. Persian Gulf War, 1991—Veterans—Medical care—
United States.   2. Persian Gulf syndrome—Political aspects.
3. Veterans— Medical care—United States.   I. Title.
DS79.744.M44H37   1998
956.7044'27—dc21   98-7645
                                                    CIP

Text design by Holly Johnson

Cover design and illustration by Ruth Ross

Manufactured in the United States of America

First Edition: June 1998

10   9   8   7   6   5   4   3   2

OATH OF OFFICE

I, *(Name)*, having been appointed an officer in the Army of the United States . . . In the grade of *(Grade)*, do solemnly swear (or affirm) that I will support and defend the Constitution of the United States against all enemies, foreign and domestic; that I will bear true faith and allegiance to the same; that I take this obligation freely, without any mental reservation or purpose of evasion; and that I will well and faithfully discharge the duties of the office upon which I am about to enter; SO HELP ME GOD.

1

The Perfect War

IT WAS THE perfect war, watched around the world on television. Five weeks of high-precision bombing and four days of ground assault, seemingly executed without flaw, and the United States military drove the Iraqis out of Kuwait in early 1991, humbled Saddam Hussein, and restored the integrity of the American GI.

The two army officers who ran the Gulf War, Colin Powell, chairman of the Joint Chiefs of Staff, and Norman Schwarzkopf, the battlefield commander, became America's first military heroes since General Douglas MacArthur in the Korean War. Saddam Hussein's regime survived, but his vaunted army had been shredded in battle by American soldiers and fighter pilots. U.S. battlefield casualties had been extremely light—only 147 were killed in combat. The stigma of Vietnam had finally been removed. "We had given America a clear win at low casualties in a noble cause," Powell wrote in *My American Journey*, his 1995 memoir, "and the American people fell in love again with their armed forces."

America celebrated with a ticker-tape parade down

Broadway. The memoirs of General Powell and General Schwarzkopf became huge best-sellers; the two generals, both retired by 1993, became America's most highly sought, and highly paid, public speakers. Powell was considered a serious candidate for the 1996 Republican presidential nomination, at least by the press and public opinion polls, until he withdrew his name from candidacy.

There were only a few glitches to the otherwise seamless acceptance of the military victory in the Gulf War:

- The American-made Patriot antimissile system, credited during the war with saving Israel from massive destruction by intercepting and destroying dozens of Iraqi Scud missiles, was determined by Israeli intelligence to have shot down, at best, only one.
- American aircraft and Special Forces units, credited by Powell and Schwarzkopf during the war with locating and demolishing most of Iraq's fleet of mobile Scud launchers, had destroyed none.
- At least thirty-five American combat deaths, one fourth of the total, were the result of errant American bombings and artillery attacks—so-called friendly-fire incidents.
- The success rate of American "smart bombs," whose devastating effect was depicted in ghostly, computer-game-like video footage during the war—and validated by on-the-scene reports from CNN correspondents in Baghdad—was found to be vastly overstated. The General Accounting Office (GAO) concluded in 1997 that the hit rate of smart bombs dropped by F117s, the hailed Stealth bomber, ranged from 41 to 60 percent. More significantly, the GAO report added that in terms of hit-

ting targets, there was little difference between the expensive high-tech bombs and those without guidance systems.

After the war, a few academics and retired military officers published analyses raising disturbing—if little-noted—questions about the intelligence assumptions underlying much of the war planning:

• The Iraqi army, which triggered the crisis by seizing Kuwait in August 1990, was much smaller and far less cohesive and formidable than thought.
• The evidence suggesting that Saddam Hussein planned to follow his occupation of Kuwait by invading Saudi Arabia and seizing its oil fields was far less categorical than as presented to the public by President George Bush.
• The Iraqi regime was and continues to be, without question, a brutal violator of human rights, but some of the most highly publicized accusations after the takeover of Kuwait—for example, that Iraqi soldiers forced nurses to remove newly born infants from their hospital incubators, consigning them to death—were found to be deliberate lies, products of a well-financed Kuwait propaganda operation in the United States.
• Much criticism revolved around the censorship that the Pentagon successfully imposed on American journalists covering the war, and the ready acceptance of those restraints by the press corps. The major television networks were adjudged to be the worst offenders: Every night Americans were fed a view of the Gulf War that

essentially was shaped by public-relations experts in the White House and the Pentagon.

The complaints, by and large, were the stuff of little-noticed congressional reports and academic journals; the public's perception of sheer success in the Gulf War could not be undone by after-the-fact naysayers. It was our Teflon war.

THE GLOSS WAS finally marred not by critics, but by the men and women who fought in the war and who remained loyal to its causes, its leaders, and its success.

What happened was simple enough: Beginning in the fall of 1991, veterans, primarily members of reserve or National Guard units, began getting sick with a variety of vague but debilitating symptoms, including rashes, stomach distress, and memory loss. Some victims said they had first noticed the ailments while on duty in the Gulf; others reported the onset after their return home. Some family members also reported similar symptoms. Naturally, the GIs turned to military doctors and Veterans Administration hospitals for help. However, the initial reponse of the military medical system was to turn away, characterizing the illnesses as having absolutely nothing to do with service in the Gulf. Word filtered down the military chain of command suggesting that those who complained were reserve or National Guard malingerers and malcontents—men and women who could not handle the stress of combat as readily as those committed to full-time service in the army, marines, navy, and air force. By early 1993, with more than four thousand Gulf War veterans reporting symptoms and the numbers steadily mounting, VA doctors were telling GIs that they were suffering from "psychological stress"—a phrase that, as most in the Pentagon understood, was considered by soldiers to be synonymous with "cowardliness." A few veterans were handed a supply of the drug Prozac by military doctors and told to return in three months; the antidepressant replaced aspirin, a World War II staple, as an all-purpose medicine. Only a few reporters and a few members of Congress and their staff cared.

By the mid-1990s, the trickle of ill and complaining GIs had turned into a well-organized tide of protesters who were convinced that the military services had placed their renewed reputation as warriors above any obligation to take care of their own troops. It had happened before: The military resisted efforts for more than twenty years to authorize benefits for Vietnam War veterans who suffered from exposure to toxic defoliants, whose most dangerous ingredient was a herbicide known as Agent Orange—made up, in part, of dioxins—used to clear the jungle in the Vietnam War. The impasse over Agent Orange came to an end in the mid-1990s only after Congress mandated that the Veterans Administration seek an independent opinion from the prestigious National Academy of Science. After a long study, the academy concluded that exposure to dioxins was associated with many types of cancer and other illnesses, and the VA agreed to provide disability and death compensation to Vietnam veterans who developed the illnesses—even decades after returning from Vietnam. The Pentagon, although confronted with a clear precedent, still was unable to listen to the Gulf War veterans. Once again, it was left to some members of Congress, responding to intense lobbying from veterans' groups, to keep alive the issue of who was sick and how they got that way. The First Lady, Hillary Clinton, eventually intervened, and a presidential advisory committee came into being in 1996 to investigate the mysterious Gulf War illness. The committee was highly critical of the military's handling of the crisis, but its essential conclusion, to the anger and dismay of the veterans, was to echo the Pentagon in concluding that the sick GIs were suffering from stress. The White House of Bill Clinton, who was privately reviled by many senior officers in the military as a Vietnam War draft dodger and an advocate of gays in the military, was no match for a Pentagon that did not want to come to terms with the real cost of the Gulf War.

At this writing, in the spring of 1998, more than ninety thousand Gulf War veterans—15 percent of those sent to war—have reported some degree of physical distress stemming, so they are convinced, from exposure to *something* while they were on active duty. In hearings in February 1998 before a House subcommittee, government health officials finally acknowledged that the initial diagnosis of stress may have been inaccurate and that some agent or series of agents—no one knew quite what—was responsible for making the GIs in the Gulf sick. Stress clearly was a factor, but it was not the sole causal agent. The subcommittee was told that the military would begin studying specific treatments for the various symptoms of Gulf War syndrome. Until then, federal research had concentrated on funding studies investigating the *causes* of the various illnesses rather than their possible cure.

W HAT WAS CAUSING the huge number of illnesses? The immediate suspects were those chemical and biological agents, odorless and silent weapons of terror, known or suspected to be in Saddam Hussein's arsenal. The most lethal chemical agents are nerve gases that work by disrupting the metabolic process and inhibiting a key enzyme needed to control muscle movement. Within a minute, the body, in essence, strangles in its own vital organs. Iraq had stockpiles of three such agents—sarin, soman, and VX. Biological agents are virulent diseases that can be mass-produced and disseminated, as a liquid or as dry spores, in quantities sufficient to trigger acute sickness over huge areas. The agent of choice for Iraq was assumed to be pulmonary anthrax, the most efficient of the highly contagious bacterial diseases. Anthrax, which was one of the plagues of medieval days, has an incubation period of less than twenty-four hours and can be up to 100 percent fatal. Iraq also was known to be doing research on lethal toxins, highly charged chemical by-products of plants and animal microorganisms that kill on contact. Eight ounces of one such by-product, botulinum toxin, was considered by American military scientists in the 1960s to be theoretically capable of wiping out the world's population.

Did the American bombing of Iraq's chemical and biological manufacturing facilities and storage depots inadvertently release germs, gases, or other toxic materials, leading to low-level exposure that may have had more damaging effects than previously known? Did the vaccines and medications provided to soldiers to help them survive a nerve gas or anthrax attack reduce resistance to low-level exposure to those very agents? Were GIs contaminated by fallout from the widespread American use against the Iraqis—for the first time in warfare—of antitank shells and bombs made from depleted uranium, a radioactive heavy metal that burns on contact?

The medical mystery behind Gulf War syndrome is a complex epidemiological maze that will take years to fully unravel, if ever. But a sick soldier or sailor is sick, whether due to stress or to some obscure illness that defies immediate diagnosis. Why did the system fail the Gulf War veterans? Did national heroes such as Norman Schwarzkopf and Colin Powell, who were known during their careers for taking care of their troops, have an obligation to speak out on behalf of the veterans—as many sick GIs believe—and demand that America's military hospitals stop turning them away?

The unsettling fact is that the Gulf War was far more costly to the United States than the Pentagon and its former leaders are willing to acknowledge. Well over one hundred thousand Gulf War veterans have registered thus far for physical examinations at Pentagon and VA clinics, with nearly 90 percent reporting some symptoms. Those men and women are friendly-fire casualties just as surely as if they had been fired upon by their fellow soldiers. The military's inevitable dilemma is profound: Can it protect our soldiers and sailors in future wars if it was unable to do so in the Gulf War?

American soldiers were spared from Iraqi bullets and artillery shells in the Gulf War, but not from toxic gases, mysterious viruses, and unknown disease. For all of their brave talk about future warfare, the men who run America's military have been unwilling—perhaps even unable—to learn the real lessons of the Gulf War.

Colin Powell, for one, professes no second thoughts about his role in the Gulf War. "We did everything we could to try to protect our troops," he said in an interview for this book. "We had a lot of folks running their mouths [before the war] and saying twenty thousand will be killed. Well, less than five hundred were killed"—in the war and as noncombatants. "It's a remarkable achievement." Asked about the veterans suffering in the aftermath of the war, Powell said, "We are still not sure if there is a Gulf War syndrome. You can scream and shout about it, but there is no answer." Powell told me that he agrees that the United States has an obligation to take care of its ailing veterans, no matter what the cause of their illness, but added that his responsibilities ended upon his retirement from the army in the fall of 1993. "If there are still some veterans who say I should have done more or said more," Powell said, "my answer is, I wasn't in the government."

DESPITE WASHINGTON'S USUAL reverential blather about America's war veterans, public debate over Gulf War syndrome has been marked by polarization and mutual recrimination—to the detriment of the veterans. Many in the Congress and the veterans' groups are convinced that the suffering GIs are victims of a huge cover-up orchestrated by the military and political leaders of the war. The Pentagon, on the other hand, sees its opponents in Congress as corrupt and cynical in their use of the Gulf veterans and the press for political purposes.

Congressional doubts about the Pentagon seemed to be validated in mid-1996 when the Pentagon acknowledged that it had overlooked intelligence dating back to the fall of 1991 noting that a huge Iraqi munitions depot at Khamisiyah, which was destroyed by American troops shortly after the war, had contained artillery shells filled with sarin. Analysts at the Central Intelligence Agency later concluded that as many as a hundred thousand American troops were in the path of the subsequent thermal plume. The delayed revelation provoked inevitable comparisons with the lying that marked so much official military reporting during the Vietnam War.

However, as I have found in my reporting for this book, the motivations behind the military's inability to deal with Gulf War syndrome are far too complex to be explained away merely as a high-level cover-up. The fact that Iraq had stored nerve gas weapons at Khamisiyah was not known to Generals Powell and Schwarzkopf, so they have emphatically told me—and there is no reason to doubt their word. There also is no evidence that *any* senior officer knew of the existence of nerve agents at Khamisiyah before or immediately after its destruction; nor is there any evidence that the soldiers involved in the actual demolition reported any immediate symptoms of nerve gas poisoning. Even the military's harshest critics in the Gulf War veterans' groups and Congress acknowledge that no American commander would ignore firm evidence of nerve gas exposure and thus put his troops at risk.

The importance of Khamisiyah was not that it was knowingly covered up, but that it *happened*—that American troops responsible for destroying Iraqi weaponry, as was being done at scores of sites after the Gulf War victory, did not *know* they were dealing with nerve gas munitions. It's what the military commanders did *not* know in early 1991 that is important. They had no clue as to the extent to which Iraq had weaponized its arsenal of chemical and biological agents, or where all the weapons that did exist were stored.

In their memoirs, Powell and Schwarzkopf briefly described their concern about Iraq's chemical and biological warfare capability, but they gave no hint of the *depth* of the Americans' concern. The men running the war were far more frightened by the specter of biological warfare than has been made public. Adding to the American fear was the certain knowledge that the United States had no effective defense against such an attack, and the distressing understanding that Iraq did not need a sophisticated delivery system to cause hundreds of thousands of American casualties.

The military's strong fears about a chemical or biological warfare terror attack could only have been soothed by an enormous sense of relief when the attack did not come, and the war against Iraq turned into one of America's finest military moments since the end of the Vietnam War. There were no mass casualties, and the thousands of body bags and pallets of elaborate medical equipment were returned, unused, after the war. The aches and pains of the Gulf War GIs seemed insignificant when compared to what they might have been. The inability of America's military leaders to deal openly and rationally with the victims of Gulf War syndrome can be more fully understood, perhaps, after a more complete account of the biological warfare scare.

2

The Scare

LARRY R. SEAQUIST will never forget his sense of despair and dread as the ground war, code-named Desert Storm, got under way early on February 24. He had gone to bed the night before convinced that he and his colleagues had not done all they could to protect American troops from an Iraqi biological warfare attack. There was a good chance that Saddam Hussein would respond to the American assault on Kuwait by sending an air force plane, spraying anthrax, on a one-way suicide mission over U.S. troop positions. There would be tens of thousands of casualties—a number so great, Seaquist believed, and so enraging to the American public that no response, not even the use of a nuclear bomb, could be ruled out.

Seaquist, a navy captain on duty at the Pentagon, was not alone in his fears. He had been at work for months on a specially assembled team that had been pulled together by Richard Cheney, the secretary of defense, and told to find a way to neutralize a possible Iraqi biological warfare attack with anthrax, or the even more deadly botulinum toxin.

Worry that Saddam Hussein would resort to such drastic means had ricocheted all fall through the White House and at the top of the Defense Department. The fear was compounded, Seaquist told me in a series of interviews, by a lack of intelligence. No one in Washington knew precisely what virulent materials had been developed in Iraq. What *was* known was politically explosive: In the mid-1980s a privately owned laboratory in suburban Washington, the American Type Culture Collection, began exporting dozens of batches of deadly anthrax cultures and other pathogens, with licensing from the Department of Commerce, to the Iraqi Atomic Energy Commission and other agencies in Iraq. The shipments came at the height of the Iran-Iraq war, when the Reagan administration's foreign policy covertly tilted toward Iraq. The Bush administration continued the tilt, and military matériel from Washington to Iraq was in the pipeline as late as January 1991, when the tilt had completely reversed and the air war against Iraq had begun. The American press, caught up in its enthusiasm for the war, did not report on those shipments at the time, although many were in the public record.

On the eve of the conflict, however, germ warfare was still very much a theoretical threat, while chemical warfare was a known weapon of choice for Iraq. Baghdad had repeatedly ignored the international taboo against such materials in its decade-long war with Iran, using both mustard gas and nerve agents. And in early 1988 Saddam Hussein ordered a savage mustard gas attack on a heavily populated Kurdish city in northern Iraq, leaving more than four thousand severely burned and maimed victims. The vast majority of the victims were noncombatants. The Bush administration also had some responsibility for the vigor of the Iraqi chemical arsenal; its covert foreign policy in the 1980s led it to secretly supply Saddam Hussein's regime with thousands of gallons of the chemicals needed for the manufacture of nerve agents.

Many journalists wrote and televised stories, as the Gulf War drew near, describing Washington's fear of a chemical or biological attack. It was that worry that led Secretary of State James A. Baker to meet with Tariq Aziz, the Iraqi foreign minister, in Geneva in early 1991, a few days before the air war, and warn in a letter meant for Saddam Hussein that Iraq would pay "a terrible price" if chemical or biological weapons were used against American troops. The Bush administration, without saying as much, wanted the Iraqi leader to believe that any use of chemicals or biologicals could trigger a nuclear response.

What the men running the government knew, and the Washington press corps and the public did not, were some of the facts put together by Larry Seaquist and his Pentagon colleagues indicating serious Iraqi planning for biological warfare in the Gulf. An elite American Special Forces team, operating deep inside Iraq before the war, had kidnapped some Iraqi soldiers and determined, from blood samples, that they had recently built up an immunity to anthrax, the most efficacious of potential biological warfare agents. It was not clear whether the Iraqis had been inoculated with anthrax vaccine or had developed immunity to the disease, which occurs naturally in the animal population in some areas of Iraq. It didn't matter. Military planning had to assume the worst-case scenario—that the Iraqis would not be affected by a biological attack. There was another finding, also very troubling. Before its invasion of Kuwait, the Iraqis had purchased some highly efficient agricultural sprayers from Italy—devices that were essential for the airborne spread of germs. The intelligence community also had detected a group of tethered goats, apparently used in testing, near a suspected biological warfare research facility. The closely held information was riveting and stressful. "We had to make the assumption," Seaquist recalled, "that Iraq had biological warfare agents—and they were weaponized." There were no defenses against anthrax—few of the American soldiers in the Gulf had been immunized—and the airborne dissemination of anthrax under the right circumstances could result in an estimated 200,000 American casualties. It was a nightmare scenario.

Anthrax could be spread from canisters strapped to the wings of an Iraqi warplane or, depending on prevailing winds, mounted on speedboats in the Persian Gulf. "Assuming the use of anthrax," Seaquist said, "there would be a ninety percent kill of *everything*" in the path of the aerosol. A U.S. Navy biological laboratory near Cairo was told to prepare for a quick diagnosis in case of biological attack, Seaquist added, and was geared to speedily analyze tissue samples from infected soldiers. If anthrax or any other lethal agent was found, the samples would be flown to Washington—a military aircraft had been put on twenty-four-hour standby in anticipation—for further confirmation. The goal of all this was to ensure, Seaquist said he was told, that "if the president nuked Baghdad" in retaliation, "he would have the capability to prove" Iraqi use of biological war.

The Pentagon's ad hoc biological warfare team included George T. Raach, an army colonel, and Bill Inglee, a deputy assistant secretary of defense. The men consulted regularly with

Billy Richardson, the deputy assistant to Dick Cheney for chemical matters. The man in charge was I. Lewis Libby, the deputy undersecretary of defense for strategy and resources, a trusted insider. Libby's marching orders were daunting: The team members could not rest until they were ready to tell the mothers of any American soldiers infected with anthrax that they had done all they could to protect their children.

Adding to the tension, George Raach recalled in an interview, was the seeming irrationality of Saddam Hussein, who made no diplomatic moves in the fall of 1990 as the United States and its coalition allies steadily augmented their forces in the Gulf. "Nobody could figure out why he was just sitting there," Raach told me, "waiting to get the shit kicked out of him. We were worried because he didn't know what he was doing. Everybody thought his guys would inflict a price." Billy Richardson, who had the most experience with germs and gases of the men at the top—he served five years in the 1980s as technical director of the army's chemical and biological defense command—told me that he came to the Pentagon every morning in the weeks before the war "wondering whether we'd be hit with a strike."

Another reason for worry was the lack of firm intelligence about the location and size of Iraq's chemical and biological arsenal. In interviews for this book, Libby's team still had sharply contradictory recollections of Iraqi capability. Seaquist recalled a briefing before the war in which it was suggested that as much as 40 percent of the Iraqi bombs and shells stockpiled in the Kuwaiti war zone could be "volumetric"—that is, capable of carrying a liquid chemical or biological payload. That estimate turned out after the war to be much too high, Seaquist noted. But Raach recalled far lower prewar estimates, some stating that no more than 5 percent of the Iraqi arsenal was chemical or biological, with no such weapons stockpiled near the Kuwaiti front. The lack of firm information led Secretary Cheney to ask his counterparts in the Soviet Ministry of Defense for their best assessment. Cheney was told that the Iraqis had not yet weaponized their virulent biological materials. (The Russians were wrong, as a United Nations inspection team determined after the war.)

Lewis Libby, whose nickname is "Scooter," worried more about the location of Iraqi chemical and biological warheads than he did about their numbers. "Whatever was there, was there," he told me. His concern, he added, was about those warheads stockpiled by Saddam Hussein in southern Iraq, close to the Kuwaiti war zone. "If he changed his mind" and decided not to use such weapons, Libby said, "it would have been hard for him to get them out. It's not easy to truck them out" when the American and coalition air forces were doing intensive bombing around the clock. Libby's fear was that Hussein might decide the war was going badly and that "he couldn't afford to lose the war. Then he'd use it and sue for peace."

One solution was to place the known and suspected chemical and biological weapons sites high on the air force's target list. That list, according to William A. Arkin, an independent defense analyst who has had access to classified data, was comprised of thirteen suspected biological warfare facilities, including three production plants, and twenty-five chemical storage and production targets. (Khamisiyah was not on the original target list.) Libby's team sought out weapons experts from the Defense Intelligence Agency—the same agency that could not say for sure where Iraq was storing its chemical and biological weapons—and was reassured, as George Raach recalled, that "the heat and the blast" from bombs would dissipate the lethal materials. "We were told that there was no danger to the United States or coalition forces in the ground or in the air."

In *Crusade*, his account of the Gulf War, *Washington Post* journalist Rick Atkinson described a high-level meeting in which General Charles A. Horner, the air force commander, abruptly cut off a debate about the perils of bombing biological and chemical warfare sites by declaring that "if there's collateral damage in Iraq perhaps that's not all bad. There has to be a penalty for building and storing these weapons. If there is some fallout in Iraq and it causes death, that penalty also sends a signal to others." The most important Iraqi chemical and biological facilities were to the north, near Baghdad, more than three hundred miles from the Kuwaiti border.

The possibility of that fallout blowing south and eventually enveloping American GIs was apparently not considered a serious deterrent by the top commanders, who were convinced that the most prudent move in terms of potential American casualties was to destroy the weapons—and deny them to Saddam Hussein. In his memoir, Colin Powell wrote of telling President Bush that "there was a risk in hitting these plants. The bombing would probably destroy any disease agents present. But it might also release them. It was a gamble, I told the President, but one we had to take. He was already agitated, and this added worry did not soothe him."

It was a decision, Powell told me when interviewed for this book, that he would make again. In his memoir, Powell seemed almost jaunty about the risk of bombing Iraq's biological production plants and "unleashing rather than preventing a catastrophe." He quoted himself as telling a British commander, speaking of the toxic cloud that could result, "If it heads south, just blame me."

Powell's real feelings, of course—and those of his fellow commanders—were anything but casual. In his memoir, the army general noted that "the wild card in this conflict was whether or not the Iraqis might resort to germ warfare. . . . The biologicals worried me, and the impact on the public the first time the first casualty keeled over to germ warfare would be terrifying." Some of the men assigned to Scooter Libby's ad hoc team came to understand that chemical and biological weapons provoked the kind of risks and consequences that senior officers find distasteful. "They really are warriors," Bill Inglee said of the top brass. "They believe in fighting by the rules. Chemicals and biologicals are dirty." Inglee, who is now a foreign policy analyst for the House Appropriations Committee, concluded that the military simply did not "want to have to fight in that environment. Who would?"

There was something both energizing and horrifying about his months on the Libby team, Inglee told me. "It felt like you were getting a window into the future of the war, and it made the hair stand up on your neck."

THREATENING SADDAM HUSSEIN and bombing his chemical and biological warfare facilities were only part of the solution. Libby's team also began scrambling that fall to find improved methods of protecting individual American and coalition soldiers. It was impossible, the men quickly learned, to produce enough vaccine in the few weeks left before the war to protect the more than six hundred thousand personnel who were in or en route to the Gulf. A viable vaccine for anthrax was available, but there was not enough: Only about a quarter of American soldiers going to the Gulf would be inoculated by early 1991.

There was another complication: In late 1990 the intelligence community concluded that Iraq had developed the capability of mass-producing botulinum toxin, the biological warfare agent estimated to be three million times more lethal than some nerve agents. There had never been a huge demand for the vaccine against botulinum. An experimental vaccine had been developed in the early 1970s, but the existing stockpiles were nearly twenty years old and had been kept under refrigeration. Larry Seaquist and two of his colleagues made a secret trip to London and conferred there with British biological warfare experts in an effort to find some means of mass-producing an effective vaccine. It wasn't possible, and only eight thousand doses of the vaccine were on hand when the American bombing of Baghdad got under way.* Another

---

*The question of who would get the limited doses of antitoxin vaccine got sticky. Rick Atkinson reports that Sir Peter de la Billière, the British commander in the Gulf War, wanted vaccine for his troops. And General Khalid bin Sultan, who commanded the Saudi troops, sought vaccine on behalf of the royal family. Schwarzkopf, wrote Atkinson, asked for guidance from Washington and "was told to make the decision himself." The general was infuriated by the response and accused the policymakers in Washington of "washing their hands like Pontius Pilate." Schwarzkopf's own staff, added Atkinson, displeased their boss by recommending that "those in critical positions" at the command post in Saudi Arabia also be given the shots. In the end, the vaccines were given to some Special Forces units and other soldiers deemed likely to be exposed to Iraqi biological warfare.

complication was the fact that the vaccine was not approved for use by the Food and Drug Administration (FDA). The Pentagon persuaded the FDA to relax its protocols, and the few doses available were distributed, on a very selective basis, before the Gulf War.

Defending against chemical warfare agents seemed easier, Larry Seaquist recalled: "You put your mask on." That issue soon became much more complicated, too. The American gas masks were difficult to fit and not as effective as those manufactured by other nations, especially those made in Russia. Subsequent Pentagon surveys, which remain classified as of today, revealed widespread dissatisfaction by GIs with the American-made gas masks. One study indicated that as many as 47 percent of the masks could not be made to work properly in the field. There were similar complaints, also still classified, about the military's cumbersome chemical protective gear, activated-charcoal outer garments designed to provide full body coverage. To make matters worse, Seaquist and his colleagues also came to realize that the chemical and biological detection devices designed for battlefield use had an essential flaw: They were capable of making determinations only *after* the fact—that is, after soldiers and sailors had been breathing the questionable air. "The technology for battlefield detection," Seaquist told me, "isn't there yet. The best chemical and biological warfare detector is a dead soldier."

It was this certain knowledge, perhaps, that drove the Pentagon to once again turn to the FDA and seek its approval for the widespread use of an experimental drug known as pyridostigmine bromide (PB), which when combined with atropine and another chemical provided an antidote against soman, a nerve agent believed to be in the Iraqi arsenal. Under the law, PB could not be administered to individuals, even GIs in a combat zone, unless there was informed consent—that is, unless the recipient was told of the drug's potential risks and benefits. The drug's efficacy as an antidote for nerve gas had been studied only in animals. There was evidence that PB, when given in high doses to healthy humans—as it would be in the Gulf War—triggered a neurological response known as bromide intoxication, the symptoms of which included confusion, tremor, memory loss, stupor, and coma. After months of debate in the fall of 1990, the FDA waived its restrictions upon being assured by the Pentagon that it would provide appropriate information about PB to all military personnel.

That promise was not kept, and the pills were handed out to all soldiers. They were to be taken—with no questions asked.

WASHINGTON'S FEAR OF a nerve gas attack had more of an impact than previously known on the military planning for the counteroffensive aimed at destroying the remnants of Saddam Hussein's once-feared Republican Guard, the most elite units in the Iraqi Army. A limited counteroffensive was to begin once Saddam Hussein's troops were ousted from Kuwait. The American plan, as finally worked out, called for the combat divisions of the VII Corps to roll into Iraq from the west in a flanking maneuver. The plan was altered at the last minute to permit two of the corps's armored divisions to relocate farther west, away from the heavier concentration of attacking American and coalition troops. The goal was to isolate the fast-moving tank units from a possible chemical warfare attack.

The successful attack, met by only token opposition, was abruptly called off by President Bush early on the war's fifth day, as the retreating Iraqis were being pummeled by around-the-clock American air strikes. The Bush administration was convinced—wrongly—that Saddam Hussein would be overthrown in the aftermath of his defeat, and there was no need, therefore, to carry the war to Baghdad.

"Chemicals were more of a consideration [in planning the counteroffensive] than most people thought," Ronald Griffith, who was then commanding general of the First Armored Division, told me. He said he and a fellow armored-division commander realized the peril "if we were bunched up [on the battlefield] and got hit with chemicals." It was at their initiative, Griffith said, that the two tank divisions were given permission to fan out west, deeper into the desert.

Griffith, who retired in 1997 as the army's vice chief of staff, recalled that when "we went into Iraq we went in absolutely convinced that we were going to encounter chemical warfare." He and his fellow officers, he added, were told that nerve agents and mustard gas had been deployed on the battlefields inside Iraq and that Saddam Hussein had delegated authority for their use to his battlefield commanders. "All of us said they're going to hit us. It was a *fait accompli*. So let's minimize the damage they can do to us."

However, the Iraqis did not use chemical weapons, Griffith said, and "we owned the battlefield."

LARRY SEAQUIST KNEW, on the eve of the ground war, that the American and coalition troops were operating with gas masks that, all too often, would not work as directed; with poorly designed warning systems for chemical and biological contamination; and, in many cases, with no effective antidotes or vaccines. "I went home the night before we attacked and assumed that we would lose thousands of men," Seaquist, who now directs an independent Washington think tank, told me. "We all believed that we had not met the Libby test: We had not done everything we could to protect our troops."

The Libby task force understood that the decision to distribute PB pills and the various vaccines was a desperation measure designed for public consumption in case of Iraqi use of chemical or biological agents. "We all knew what would happen, in terms of public response," George Raach told me, "if an attack came and we didn't have the stuff. I remember discussions with someone saying, 'We don't want another Agent Orange here.' "

Scooter Libby, now a Washington attorney, believes that there were profound issues raised by his ad hoc task force prior to the Gulf War. "People have to learn that biological warfare is no different than nuclear warfare," Libby told me. "The world we are entering now has the capability for fifty nations to be 'nuclear' "—by developing the easier-to-produce and much less expensive biological weaponry. "They have production capability and the means for delivery."

At the time, of course, Libby's task force and the data it

collected were highly secret. Libby, asked about the secrecy, had a ready and sensible justification: "Why teach him [Saddam Hussein] what frightens us?"

But there are more difficult questions that should have been posed at higher levels in the government. Former senator David Boren of Oklahoma, a Democrat who was the widely respected chairman of the Senate Intelligence Committee in 1990, recalls little more than a generalized briefing on Iraq's biological capability in the weeks before the Senate narrowly voted, 52 to 47, in support of George Bush's use of force against Saddam Hussein. "I'm positive that no meeting of the Intelligence Committee took place to discuss biological warfare as a separate subject," Boren, now president of the University of Oklahoma, told me. The subject did not arise during the floor debate before the January 12, 1991, Senate vote. He did vaguely recall, Boren added, that "someone somewhere talked about it, but not in a major way."

Should the Senate have been told of the Bush administration's concerns about Iraqi use of biological warfare—and what weapons the United States would use to respond to such an attack? Should the Senate have been told, before its vote, what Libby's people knew—that kidnapped Iraqi soldiers were carrying anthrax antibodies? Should it have been told that America's defenses against chemical and biological warfare were at best suspect and at worst liable to cause illness? Should it have been told all the risks?

3

The Veterans

THE STORIES BEGAN to emerge, ever so slowly, in the months after the war. No one, especially in the U.S. government, paid much attention. Norman Schwarzkopf had retired to a new life as an authentic hero and author. Colin Powell would soon do the same. Some of the Gulf War veterans had retired, too, but their old life had come into retirement with them—in the form of debilitating disease.

Their stories, as provided in interviews and before congressional committees, are accounts of excruciating hardships and official neglect. The impact of Gulf War syndrome cannot be understood without their testimony.

KIMO S. HOLLINGSWORTH of Shepherdstown, West Virginia, was deployed to the Gulf as a marine lieutenant in September 1991 and served as a platoon commander during the liberation of Kuwait. Before going to war, he told a

House committee in 1996, "I was in excellent physical condition." He was released from active duty in May 1992. His only physical complaint at the time was a "postnasal drip and the coughing up of dark sputum which I dismissed as bad sinus problems." He took a job as a financial consultant with a Wall Street brokerage firm in July 1992 and four months later came down with "what I thought was a severe case of the flu." Within weeks, his health became progressively worse, with the following major symptoms: severe constant headaches; severe muscle and joint pain; sharp pain in the center chest; increased coughing of dark green sputum, now in hardened chunks; severe increase in urination; periodic blurred vision; memory loss; and low-grade fever.

"Despite my symptoms," Hollingsworth related, "the VA hospital in Washington performed a complete physical and concluded that I was in excellent health. The VA doctor informed me that the dark green chunks of sputum and pain in the center chest were normal in some people. I was then directed to a social worker who discussed the issue of posttraumatic stress disorder. The VA also provided me [with] a brochure outlining psychological counseling services available to Persian Gulf veterans."

Hollingsworth turned to a private physician for help and was treated with massive amounts of antibiotics. He eventually regained 80 to 90 percent of his health. "As an American who volunteered to serve my country," Hollingsworth told the committee, "I can accept bad medical news. What I cannot accept and will not tolerate are professional bureaucrats that first deny a problem exists, then minimize problems once they surface, and lastly make the problems seem more complex so endless studies can be conducted. . . . The

Department of Defense must learn that young men and women of this country are a valuable resource. I am a combat veteran, not an expendable item."

JERRY WHEAT OF Albuquerque, New Mexico, joined the army in 1987 and served as a cavalry scout for the Third Armored Division during the Gulf War. He was injured in a friendly-fire incident during heavy fighting near the Iraqi border on February 26, the third day of the ground war, when his vehicle was struck by depleted-uranium rounds fired by an American tank. He received a Purple Heart for his shrapnel wounds.

Wheat, speaking at a news conference in early 1998 organized by a veterans' rights group, told of first becoming ill in October of 1991: "I began having abdominal pains that would drop me to the floor, and I could barely eat. This went on for several weeks even though I was seeing a doctor at an air force hospital in Albuquerque, New Mexico. I left the military shortly after falling ill. . . . I contemplated suicide because there were no answers and there was no treatment.

"Later on, I visited the VA in Albuquerque, and I was told that the illnesses are not real, but that it is psychological—that it is in my mind." In March of 1992, Wheat recounted, his father, an industrial technician at Los Alamos National Laboratory, where the atomic bomb was developed, "called me and informed me that the shrapnel taken by my gear and skin were radioactive. This was a tremendous surprise to me, since the army never bothered to tell me I was hit with radioactive and toxic ammunition. . . . By 1993, I had lost sixty pounds, and the VA has yet to explain this to me."

Wheat's uranium poisoning case is being followed today by a VA medical team, but the VA's program, he noted, "only follows a handful of those with known heavy doses of DU [depleted uranium] exposure. Our government should stop using depleted uranium," Wheat says. "If it won't do that, then the least it can do is . . . admit that many, many more were exposed to DU dust and begin to provide health care as soon as possible—before it is too late."

STEVE ROBERTSON OF Fredericksburg, Virginia, was forty, an old man—by army standards—when he went to the Gulf. An army reservist, he supported the war then and still supports it. He became ill with what he thought was the flu in late February 1991. Over the next two years, he was racked with constant chills, diarrhea, nausea, fever, memory loss, and aching joints. Military doctors told him he just had a bad case of the flu. He eventually visited a physician at Walter Reed Army Hospital in Washington, D.C. "He gave me Prozac," Robertson said in an interview for this book, "and said come back in ten days." Robertson did so and, upon his return, was given a prescription for more Prozac and the following advice: "Take them for ninety days and come back."

Robertson, who today is the legislative director in Washington for the American Legion, understood that Prozac was an antidepressant and was "not for joint pain." He said he told the army physician, "My pain is physical—not mental," and refused to take the pills. Nonetheless, he was later told by VA doctors that he was suffering from stress. "The only stress I had," Robertson told me, "is from those guys."

He had learned a great deal about stress, he explained, while serving as a missile launch silo officer in an earlier tour of duty with the air force. His assignment in the Gulf was benign by comparison—guarding an ammunition dump in Saudi Arabia. Nothing would ever compare, Robertson told me, with the stress of living underground in twenty-four-hour shifts and being capable of triggering the end of the world with the turn of a key. While on duty in the Gulf, Robertson said, "I read more books than ever before." There were no financial hardships, and there was frequent telephone contact with his family.

Robertson realized very shortly after he became ill that the Pentagon was going to have a major confrontation with its Gulf War veterans. Through his job with the American Legion, he was constantly coming into contact with GIs suffering, as he did, from chronic flulike symptoms, memory loss, and aching joints. They too were being assured that their problems were not physical but mental. "They couldn't get health care," Robertson told me. "Military doctors wouldn't treat them because they were not on active duty. The VA wouldn't treat them because their illness wasn't service-connected. Civilians wouldn't treat them because it *was* service-connected." In Robertson's view, the Pentagon's attitude toward its soldiers couldn't be clearer: "Salute sharply and go to the next war." He is still waiting for the VA to process his claims for benefits as a Gulf War medical victim.

"How can they give me disability," Robertson asked rhetorically, "when no one can tell me what's going on?"

The failure of the system is all the more frustrating, he added, because Gulf War syndrome gave the Pentagon and the VA medical system "a golden opportunity" to correct its past mistakes with Agent Orange and the Vietnam War veterans: "The VA could have opened its arms and said, 'We've learned our lessons.' "

Nonetheless, added Robertson, despite his aches and his misgivings, "if they said 'Steve, we need you to go back,' I'd go back—because I know we were right."

STEVEN WRAY WOOD was an all-star athlete in his youth in Florida who loved water sports. Today he says he can no longer walk a hundred yards without suffering severe side effects. "My life was changed forever," Wood, a staff sergeant in the Gulf War, told a congressional hearing in 1997. He was an army-trained specialist in nuclear, biological, and chemical defenses. In that capacity, a few days after the end of the ground war in Iraq, Wood stopped his jeep to inspect a bombed-out Iraqi munitions depot. Army demolition units were methodically destroying all weapons depots in the aftermath of the war as part of an effort to deny artillery shells and ammunition to the surviving remnants of the Republican Guard. "I witnessed a few artillery rounds," Wood testified, "that were sitting by themselves and roped off with yellow engineer tape." He subsequently identified the shells, which had Soviet markings, as chemical weapons and filed an official report about his finding. "Later that day," Wood testified, "I started to get very sick with the symptoms I suffer still today."

He immediately sought medical help but, over the next few weeks, was told it was "all in my head" and urged to get back to his military assignment. "I was a good soldier," Wood said, "and did what the doctors said, since I had always thought I could trust them. I pushed and I pushed myself until my body could go no further." By 1994 "my condition had gotten so bad I could not even remember my wife's name nor where I lived," Wood said. Army doctors were not much help. His medical retirement from the army was delayed, Wood said, "because I still had unexplained symptoms that were being called Gulf War illness. I was informed the only way my medical board [early retirement with disability payment] would be allowed to continue was if all references to these unexplained illnesses were omitted. I was exasperated and agreed. A deciding factor in this decision was my being threatened with punishment because I was physically unable to work."

After his official retirement, Wood told Congress, it took the Veterans Administration eighteen months to process his claim for compensation: VA administrators said there was no evidence that his injuries were service-connected. One VA physician concluded during those months that he might have multiple sclerosis, Wood recounted, but the VA refused to pay for needed further testing while his claim was being processed. Wood went to a private physician for the tests, which were negative. He eventually was given compensation by the VA, but not for Gulf War syndrome—he was officially listed as suffering war-related eczema.

Wood, who is married to a German citizen, decided to stay on in Germany because of its free health care. In one visit to a German clinic, he testified, the doctors "did more tests in two hours than the army did in five years." They also told him that he had been poisoned while in the army.

He came to Washington to testify, Wood told Congress in 1997, because "it is a matter of principle. I sacrificed my health for my country and would just like to be recognized for it. Now you know that the army treats its sick soldiers with total disregard."

NEIL R. TETZLAFF, of Reed City, Michigan, was serving as a lieutenant colonel on active duty in the air force when he was deployed to the Persian Gulf as a deputy commander for an F-111 fighter wing. Like all soldiers going into the war zone, he was issued a seven-day supply of PB pills and ordered to take three a day. He took his first pill on the plane en route to Saudi Arabia and promptly vomited. "I attributed the sickness to the plane ride and the tension of the situation," Tetzlaff told a Senate committee in 1994. "On my second day there I vomited again and felt different. I attributed the sickness to something I had eaten. On the third day there I was extremely nauseated and vomited many times. I sought out the doctor and discussed my illness with him. We dismissed it as something I had eaten at the Saudi canteen. On my fourth day there I vomited violently, the worst ever of my life, and was acting a bit off center and muddled. On the fifth day I didn't vomit but was sore, lost much of my bounce, acted strangely silly, and was totally out of character. On the sixth day I was incoherent, extremely tired, and at times irrational. On the morning of the seventh day I vomited about a quart of blood."

Tetzlaff was rushed to surgery and found to have a severe stomach tear, the obvious result of his vomiting. "Under ideal conditions," Tetzlaff testified, "by day three my attending physician . . . would have recognized my symptoms as an overdose of pyridostigmine" and immediately ordered an evacuation to a detoxification center. Instead, over the next two years, Tetzlaff related, military and VA doctors consistently reassured him that the PB, in the doses he received, "was a completely harmless drug." During the Gulf War, Tetzlaff found, military doctors routinely returned soldiers suffering from PB poisoning to duty without telling them to stop taking the pills. His personal medical record, as maintained by the air force, includes no entries between July 9 and September 6, 1990, the weeks in which he became ill and underwent surgery. "While I was in the VA hospital," Tetzlaff said, "several Gulf War veterans related that they were astonished by the healthy young people who died of heart attacks. They were amazed that no investigation was accomplished; rather, these soldiers were simply stuffed into body bags and sent home." In every case, the now-retired air force colonel told Congress, "the deceased were taking pyridostigmine bromide.

"Before going to Saudi Arabia," Tetzlaff said, "I considered myself to be in excellent physical condition, as I enjoyed running three to five miles a day, worked out at the gym three times a week, and participated in a number of sports. Now I suffer from shooting pains throughout, joint and muscular pain, testicular pain, headaches, fatigue, diarrhea, sleep disorder, short-term memory problems, speech disorder, palsy, and dry cough.

"I have told the story of pyridostigmine bromide to every doctor that I have seen since I started going to VA; I did not miss a one. I told them exactly what I took and for how long I took it. They dismissed it as something that didn't happen. They have also said that all my problems I made up myself. In other words, I wanted to make my life this way. . . . As far as VA is concerned, I have a mental disorder."

4

Shoot the Messengers

M OST OF THE early complaints came from army reservists and National Guard personnel who found themselves too sick to return to their civilian jobs and civilian life.
But the individual accounts of illness and hardship, all equally
poignant, disappeared into bureaucratic indifference as Washington, and America, celebrated its wondrous triumph in the
Gulf desert.

The Pentagon's only response was to attack the messen-
gers. In scores of interviews for this book, senior officers recalled the widespread belief in late 1991 and 1992 that the
sick soldiers were malingerers who were trying to worm out
of their military assignments or weasel additional benefits.
Rear Admiral Ronald F. Marryott, who was in charge of the
day-to-day operations in the Defense Intelligence Agency at
the time of his retirement in 1991, recalled his first impres-
sion: that the complaints of illness were from "reservists who
were overreacting." He asked around, Marryott told me, and
was informed that there was "no evidence" that any GIs had

been exposed to gas attacks. Marryott, who is now president of the alumni association at the U.S. Naval Academy in Annapolis, Maryland, eventually changed his mind as more Gulf veterans came forward with their complaints. He began wondering, he said, "what did happen—if we're right in saying there was no contamination" on the battlefields. "A sick sailor is a sick sailor," Marryott added.

Commander Michael N. Pocalyko, a navy aviator, was reassigned from the Persian Gulf to a high-level staff job in the secretary of the navy's office in the early 1990s and was stunned at his colleagues' skepticism toward the sick soldiers. "I got back to the Pentagon," Pocalyko told me, "and people were saying, 'I never heard of a disease that only hits reservists from small towns.' There was an overwhelming view among the senior officers that this was psychological."

Colin Powell told me that he heard very little about Gulf War syndrome before his retirement in September 1993. While in office, he said, he did learn of a number of illnesses among the members of an army reserve or National Guard unit—he said he wasn't sure which one—in Alabama. At the time, like many of his fellow commanders in the Pentagon, Powell said, "I did not know whether people were feeding off each other's illnesses."

Even the most sophisticated of consultants saw no immediate reason for alarm. Dr. Matthew Meselson, a prize-winning molecular and cell biologist at Harvard University and a longtime adviser on chemical and biological warfare issues to the defense community, was consulted on the chemical warfare risks before the Gulf War. "We never thought there were serious consequences of low-level exposure" from the bombing of Iraqi nerve gas depots, Meselson told me. "So I always felt that maybe they [the sick Gulf War veterans] were malingering."

The attitude of the men at the top was reflected, as was inevitable, throughout the chain of command—and throughout the military medical system. A money-saving factor was at work, too. In September 1992, VA hospitals were instructed by the federal budget office, the Office of Management and Budget (OMB), to bill all veterans claiming to be Gulf War syndrome victims for any medical treatment, pending a determination by the VA that their illnesses were war-related. The Catch-22 was that the VA was denying the vast majority of such claims because there was no evidence that the illnesses resulted from the war.

R. J. Vogel, the VA's undersecretary for benefits, spelled out the conundrum in carefully worded language during testimony before the Senate Committee on Veterans' Affairs in May 1994: "We find that many claims based on exposure to environmental hazards while in the Gulf are based on exposure only, without further specification of a disability. Exposure alone does not provide a basis to grant service connection to a veteran." As of that date, Vogel added, 3,500 Gulf War veterans had filed disability claims. Less than half of those claims had been processed, and benefits were provided in only 278 cases. Vogel was never asked by the senators— and never volunteered—what percentage of those veterans whose cases were approved received only partial or minimal benefits.

The VA bureaucracy and many of its doctors, as we have seen, shared the initial skepticism of Colin Powell and Matthew Meselson, and systematically began telling veterans that they were suffering from stress and that their illness was not war-related. Those who did not—physicians, for example, who saw evidence of systemic neurological damage in the veterans—were discouraged by their superiors from recommending permanent benefits. Dr. William Baumzweiger, a neurologist and psychiatrist at a VA hospital in Los Angeles that was a referral center for Gulf War victims, was assigned in 1993 to evaluate a group of veterans. "When I saw what was to me clear signs of symptoms and history suggestive that they had been exposed to neurotoxin [nerve gas poisoning]," Baumzweiger testified at a House subcommittee hearing in 1996, his superiors at the VA told him "there was no such thing. . . . I was told that they were not exposed to neurotoxin, that it simply did not happen and I should not consider that as a possibility and I should treat them for whatever one could conventionally treat them for. . . . I was told this in no uncertain terms. And this is supposedly a [Gulf War] treatment center."

Another physician, Dr. Katherine Murray Leisure, a specialist in infectious disease, was fired in 1997 after treating more than six hundred veterans at the VA hospital in Lebanon, Pennsylvania. Her ouster came a few weeks after she sent a superior a caustic five-step outline on how to avoid providing medical care for Gulf War veterans. The steps were: (1) keep claims lost in limbo for years; (2) bill veterans for services; (3) alter diagnoses to reflect depression, stress, and postcombat fatigue; (4) ignore physical, clinical, or laboratory abnormalities in veterans and deny their presence publicly; and (5) never admit that modern medicine may be facing a new disease. "I am one of the many *refusenik* professionals," Dr. Leisure told me in a letter, "who remain deeply concerned about the integrity and efficacy of today's federal medical programs. The story of concealed medical illnesses in Gulf veterans certainly needs to be told."

IT WAS ALMOST second nature for the regular army officers to fix blame on the reserves or the National Guard, given the constant tension between the latter groups and those on active duty. Retired army major Jane E. Holl, who served in Schwarzkopf's headquarters during the war and later in the White House, told me that she initially viewed the Gulf War illnesses as a "reserve component phenomenon and not an active duty phenomenon. Once it became a reserve issue, the active duty didn't want to associate with it."

The reservists correctly perceive themselves to be second-class citizens who are called from private life during international crises, as in the Gulf War, and often given secondary missions, while the regular army units—and their commanding officers—get more glamorous combat assignments. Even today, senior army officials routinely refer to reservists in private conversations as "the Christmas help." The regular army cannot be quite as cavalier about the National Guard, whose existence dates back to the Revolutionary War and the Founding Fathers' distrust of professional military. National Guard units are essentially state militias that report to the state governors for domestic emergencies and civil missions; they can be summoned by the Pentagon only in times of international crisis. Under the law, the Pentagon can deploy the National Guard only in their preexisting units. The regular army maintains a disdain for the combat capability of Guard units and—in the view of the Guard—deprecates their performance in war and war games.

But reserve and National Guard units are far cheaper to maintain—a National Guard division can operate at one fourth the cost of a regular army division—and provide hard-to-ignore efficiency and flexibility. Major General Donald E. Edwards, the retired adjutant general of the Vermont National Guard, told me, "You could make a very good case that the army should have a few helicopter units and the rest should be in the National Guard." Edwards, who spent twelve years as an officer on active duty in the army, acknowledged with a laugh, however, that "the regular army would say that I was full of it." After retiring in 1997 from the National Guard, Edwards joined the staff of Representative Bernard Sanders of Vermont, the only political independent in Congress, to handle veterans' and military issues.

The irony, or tragedy, in all of the squabbling between the regular army and its Guard and reserve units is that—as no one knew in 1992 and 1993— the issue of who was serving in which unit when they got sick would become moot. After years of hiding symptoms, thousands of career officers and enlisted men and women began reporting their illnesses in the mid-1990s, with the same disabilities as seen earlier in reserve and National Guard troops. The careerists had good reason for their delay: The armed forces, in the midst of budget and personnel cutbacks in the first years of the Clinton administration, were drumming soldiers and sailors with Gulf War syndrome out of the service. "People in the army *still* have symptoms and keep it under wraps," explained Sara Lister, an assistant secretary of the army who began dealing with

Gulf War syndrome in 1994. "They feel it would be viewed as stress. Some officers put out the line that people who get Gulf War illness are weaker.

"A hell of a lot of soldiers lied about their illness," Lister said. "And there were some doctors who helped them cover it up because [the GIs] would be out otherwise." All of this was widely known throughout the Pentagon. "The truth is," added Lister, who left the army in 1997, that "health interests are not high-priority issues in the Pentagon."

GULF WAR SYNDROME was a low-priority health issue, but one with a capacity to diminish, in time, America's victory against Iraq. The huge numbers of seriously ill GIs demonstrated that high-tech modern warfare in the Persian Gulf, with its weapons made from depleted uranium and its germs, gases, and other environmental hazards, was equally dangerous, if not more so, as previous wars—in South Vietnam, South Korea, and the two world wars. Colin Powell's vision of the Gulf War being a "clear win at low casualties," as he wrote in his memoir, was a fantasy.

Powell's beliefs, coupled with the military's instinctive disdain for chemical and biological warfare, made it almost inevitable that he and other senior commanders would be unable to immediately grasp the significance of the unexplained ailments that began to afflict the veterans. "It is fair to say that the military inexperience with germ and gas warfare contributed to overlooking the Gulf War syndrome," explained Richard J. Danzig, a former undersecretary of the navy who is widely respected in the Pentagon for his strategic thinking and writing about biological warfare. Danzig, who left the Pentagon in 1997, was one of the few Clinton administration officials to debrief Scooter Libby about his prewar attempt to cope with anticipated Iraqi use of anthrax and toxins.

"There was a disconnect," Danzig explained in an interview, between the Libby group's "general fears about biological warfare and their ability to do anything about it." The same disconnect, he believes, persisted after the Gulf War. "You're asking military officers to deal with things [diseases] with Latin names and to work with doctors," Danzig told me. "That makes them uncomfortable."

It is understandable, Danzig added, that senior generals would find it difficult to come to grips with germs and gases as weapons of war, especially after learning that many of their soldiers may have been injured—not by bullets, but by biological agents or lingering chemical fumes. "They did not consider it," the former navy undersecretary said. "The senior military people say, 'What we do is fight. This other stuff is not my arena. It's messy. Sickness is not what I deal with.' "

5

The Intelligence

THE PENTAGON BRASS, with no understanding of the significance of Gulf War syndrome in the first years after the war, had no reason to worry about its causes. There was no careful review of the Defense Intelligence Agency's prewar findings on Iraq's chemical and biological warfare capabilities. There were no lessons learned about Iraqi special weapons—and, so the winners of the Gulf War thought, no lessons to *be* learned.

GIs told stories about chemical alarms being triggered on scores of occasions during the Gulf War, preceded, in some cases, by loud explosions and strange smells. Troops stopped whatever they were doing to immediately don gas masks and, in some cases, protective gear. Nothing happened. No soldier fell immediately ill with nerve gas or mustard gas poisoning; no soldier began to exhibit any of the symptoms of a biological attack. As a result, the alarms were considered to have been triggered by mistake or by any of the various pollutants in the desert—including the heavy smoke that resulted from the Iraqi decision, on the eve of the ground war, to begin blowing up the Kuwaiti oil fields.

The only official recognized chemical warfare casualty during the Gulf War was a hapless army private named David A. Fisher who brushed up against what apparently was a mustard agent while checking out a munitions bunker a few miles from the Kuwaiti border in southeastern Iraq. The injury took place on March 1, the day after Iraq formally surrendered in the war. Fisher suffered painful blisters on his left arm, was immediately treated for his burns, then was awarded a Purple Heart.

Word traveled fast in the desert, and within a few days the fact that a soldier had been exposed to mustard gas while investigating an Iraqi bunker was known to all. Ronald Griffith's Third Armored Division had the daunting assignment of destroying a huge Iraqi arsenal in western Iraq and, the retired general recalled, he and his subordinates were exceedingly worried about an accidental triggering of a nerve gas or mustard gas rocket. "Somebody went into a bunker and got burned," Griffith told me, referring to David Fisher, "and that was across the theater in a day."

Given the constant GI worry about chemical munitions and the ease with which bad news traveled, any attempt to cover up or mask a chemical warfare exposure was impossible. Alarms were still going off, but there were no further reports of GIs being directly exposed to chemicals. The American units finished their demolition and returned home. Under the terms of the peace agreement, Iraqi nuclear, chemical, and biological warfare facilities would now be inspected and destroyed by the United Nations Special Commission (UNSCOM), headed by a Swedish diplomat named Rolf Ekaus.

UNSCOM'S FINDINGS RIPPED huge holes in the prewar American intelligence estimates of Iraqi chemical and biological capability. These findings should have raised devastating questions about the American collection and processing of information. But no one in the Pentagon was paying attention.

The UNSCOM inspectors, many of them Americans, found chemical warfare production plants, storage facilities, and weapons depots scattered all over Iraq—more than ninety in all—that had been overlooked and were unknown, with one exception, by American intelligence. The UN inspectors had a major advantage in their work: They were on the ground in Iraq and did not have to rely, as did the Pentagon analysts, on satellite photo and communications intercepts. UNSCOM had access to what the intelligence community calls "groundspeak." There was an eerie pattern to the UN findings: In those areas targeted in the Gulf War because U.S. intelligence thought Iraqi chemical weapons were stored there, the intelligence was wrong, and in those areas targeted for other reasons that inadvertently happened to contain chemicals, the chemical munitions escaped serious damage. The one known area where American bombs and American intelligence were congruent was Iraq's main chemical warfare production plant at Muthanna, sixty-five miles northwest of Baghdad, which was a priority target of American warplanes.

Elsewhere in Iraq, the UN inspectors found 150,000 chemical munitions, some unfilled, and 590 tons of lethal agents that had been missed by American and coalition bombing attacks. More alarming, UNSCOM eventually found major biological-agent production plants, all carefully disguised, that had not been known to American intelligence, and at least seventy-five Scud warheads filled with anthrax and nerve agents, which could have been fired at targets in Israel and Saudi Arabia at any point during the war. It took four years, Rolf Ekaus said in an interview for this book, before UNSCOM was able to learn, through a defector, that Iraq had in fact found a way to weaponize anthrax. UNSCOM eventually determined that Saddam Hussein had a stockpile of at least twenty-five anthrax-filled bombs and near the war's end had brought some of those warheads to a small airfield in western Iraq, opposite the Israeli border, for what could have been a last-minute threat—or potential Götterdämmerung attack if Norman Schwarzkopf's army invaded Baghdad. "It was hair-raising," Ekaus told me.

The UN official also expressed dismay over what seemed to be American ignorance, after the peace agreement, of the dangers from stockpiled chemical weapons inside Iraq. American demolition teams had blown up and dismantled dozens of Iraqi weapons depots without taking *any* precautions against fallout. "We detected huge amounts of chemical weapons—rockets, artillery shells, and bombs—after the war," Ekaus said, "but the Americans didn't *know* they were dealing with chemical weapons." The American demolition activity "was innocent and very amateurishly done. We had to bring experts and dig ditches [before setting off high explosives]. We took environmental care." At some point in mid-1991, Ekaus added, the UN team inspected the huge depot at Khamisiyah, the site of later controversy, and found leaking and partially destroyed chemical weapons.

It was his opinion, Ekaus said, that the real ravages of Gulf War syndrome "had to do with the destruction *after* the war." The UN's findings, including a description of the chemical weapons at Khamisiyah, were made public in subsequent months, but created no public stir and no soul-searching in the Pentagon.

BILL ARKIN, WHO has closely studied the air war against Iraq—he made two trips there after the war—told me that the American intelligence community has yet to come to grips with its failures in the Gulf War. "They had a list of seventeen or nineteen suspected chemical weapons sites [in the Kuwaiti war zone] that were targeted," Arkin said, amplifying findings he published in an essay for the spring 1998 issue of *The Washington Quarterly*. "They inspected the sites at the end of the war and there was nothing there. And so it was assumed there were no weapons. It was total hubris," he said of the Gulf War intelligence command. "They wrote their own script, performed the play, and reviewed it. And so it was great."

Arkin has in his possession CIA studies, made public under the Freedom of Information Act, concluding that less than 5 percent of the huge Iraqi stockpile of chemical weapons was actually hit by American bombs during the war. The CIA analyses further showed, Arkin said, that American aircraft "never successfully hit a single location of biological weapons or agents.

"The intelligence community and Pentagon are assumed to be hiding vital information," Arkin said, referring to the attitude of many in the press, Congress, and Veterans' groups toward the Gulf War syndrome debate, "yet at the same time the records show that they were unorganized and ignorant."

THERE WAS ANOTHER major UNSCOM finding dealing with chemical and biological warfare: the fact that American bombing before and during the ground war had not prevented the Iraqis from routinely moving Scud missiles and warheads—including some filled with nerve gas and anthrax—to various launching sites. The Iraqis also were able to use Highway 10, an important east-west artery, to transfer mobile launchers for the Scuds from the western desert, close to potential targets in Israel, to the east, near Saudi Arabia and the American headquarters. "You had movement back and forth across the country during the war," Timothy McCarthy, an American arms proliferation expert who worked in Iraq for UNSCOM, said in an interview. "They simply loaded Scud missiles onto a launcher and drove hundreds of kilometers—in many cases without cover."

The Pentagon reassured the UNSCOM team that Highway 10 had been a priority target for American bombs and Special Forces troops, who completely cut off all traffic. "Yes, you are right," Iraqi officials subsequently told the inspectors, "but, sirs, there is the *old* Highway 10, just to the north, and that's what we used." McCarthy, now a senior analyst at the Center for Nonproliferation Studies in Monterey, California, said that the existence of the old highway was apparently not known to the American intelligence experts.

In one of his interviews with me, Larry Seaquist provided a footnote that could explain much of the self-delusion that marked the highly publicized American claims of total success in annihilating the Iraqi mobile launcher force. In one typical claim, made on a Sunday-morning network television show on January 20, 1991, four days after the first Scuds landed in Israel, Norman Schwarzkopf reassured the nation that American fighter planes and Special Forces units had destroyed all of Iraq's fixed Scud launchers and "as many as sixteen" of Iraq's estimated twenty mobile launchers.

What happened, Seaquist told me, was simply that the United States fell prey to Iraqi deception. "Some of the launchers we hit were decoys," Seaquist said, summarizing an intelligence finding that was disseminated after the war. The Iraqis had been instructed in the art of deception by the East Germans and had put into place a dual level of decoys. "The first level were cardboard cutouts" of mobile launchers, Seaquist learned—cutouts that were easily detected by photo interpreters. The photo intercepts learned to look for the real thing nearby, and invariably found it—an unmistakable launcher, with wheels that seemed ready to move. But it too, Seaquist said, turned out to be a fake, made of papier-mâché. The false launchers were so realistic, Seaquist was told, that "our reconnaissance photograph used by pilots of a typical mobile launcher was of a fake. The level of deception was remarkable."

The military commanders did not know the extent of the Iraqi biological warfare buildup. They did not know the location of the Iraqi chemical weapons arsenal. The chemical warfare alarms did not work as designed. Many gas masks, carried by each soldier as the first line of defense, could not be made to fit or work properly. American bombs, targeted on Iraqi biological chemical facilities, did not go where they were aimed. The possibility of low-level exposure to nerve agents from bombing and demolition was not entertained.

It was more than sloppy, and more than the normal fog of war. A veteran suffering from Gulf War syndrome could even believe it to be criminal negligence.

6

A Turning Point

THE SILENT SCREAMING of the veterans began coming to an end in September 1993, when Senator Donald W. Riegle Jr., a Democrat who had been in Congress since 1966, issued a report stating what no other responsible member of the House or Senate had yet dared to say—that Gulf War syndrome might be linked to exposure to Iraqi chemical warfare agents and biological toxins. America's glorious triumph in the Gulf might not have been as cost-free as reported.

Right or wrong, Don Riegle was impossible to easily dismiss. As chairman of the influential Committee on Banking, Housing and Urban Affairs, he had jurisdiction over the Commerce Department's export licensing policy, and he used that jurisdiction in the fall of 1992 to conduct extensive hearings into the Bush administration's tilt toward Iraq and its policy of supplying Saddam Hussein with American weapons. The hearings disclosed government licensing between 1985 and 1990 for no fewer than 771 sales to Iraq of sensitive dual-use equipment—including missile guidance gear, high-tech computers for targeting, and toxic precursor chemicals that, when mixed

together, create nerve gas. It was in the aftermath of those dis-
coveries that Riegle's committee learned that the Department
of Commerce had authorized the sale to Iraq of lethal biological pathogens, such as anthrax, suitable for military use.

And now, in 1993, Riegle was suggesting that some of those
shipments could have played a role in making thousands of
American GIs sick. Even today, five years later, the Riegle report
remains a sensitive issue in the Pentagon. "I didn't know what
the government was doing or not doing," Colin Powell told me
in the spring of 1998, with some rancor. "It blew open after I
left, when Senator Riegle wrote his famous report." He had not
known that nerve gas munitions were stored at Khamisiyah, the
huge Iraqi weapons depot, when it was destroyed after the war
by an army demolition unit. Had he known, Powell added, he
still would have ordered Khamisiyah's destruction. But, he said,
"we would have figured out the right way to do it."

The Riegle report was yet another blow in a bad summer
at the Pentagon. The army was facing a budget crunch and
was mandated to eliminate bases as well as reduce the number on active duty from more than 1 million to 495,000. The
cold war was over, but there was a crisis over a nuclear reac-
tor in North Korea. And there was a new president, who, in
the view of many senior officers, was a Vietnam War draft
dodger who advocated homosexuality in the military and
didn't know how to salute. The response to the Riegle report
was predictable: a categorical denial. The press was told that
the Gulf War was long over and there were no reports of
chemical warfare or Iraqi chemical weapons in the war zone.

The Riegle report was based on data in the public do-
main, and especially on the reports of Rolf Ekaus's UN inspection team. It was the kind of research that should have

been done by an investigative team for a major newspaper, but the Gulf War veterans had only two good friends in the press in the fall of 1993—a reporter for the *Birmingham News* named Dave Parks and Thomas D. Williams of the *Hartford Courant.* The two had written dozens of stories after being approached by local Gulf War veterans.

It was the suffering of the veterans, Don Riegle told me, as well as his knowledge of America's prewar military support for Iraq that led him into the issue. "When the sick veterans started popping up," Riegle said, "I felt we had to come to terms with the fact that Saddam Hussein had a chemical and biological warfare arsenal that we had helped him create. The clean war"—against Iraq—"wasn't a clean war for the hundred thousand or so who are sick. It's a nightmare war for them. There's been a long, inexcusable turning of the back to these people."

Riegle had strongly supported legislation in the Senate that provided retroactive benefits and medical care for veterans affected by Agent Orange in Vietnam, and he understood that the struggle for benefits would be renewed on behalf of Gulf War veterans—and once again would be difficult. "I knew the Pentagon not only won't be honest about it," he said, referring to responsibility for the Gulf War illnesses, "and they certainly won't want to pay for it or acknowledge it. So we tried to document the report as much as we could. The irony of all this is that you didn't need Perry Mason to get the answers. It isn't as if we took a lot of sick people *into* the army."

The conclusion of the thirty-four-page report was straightforward: "Thousands of American servicemen and women are reportedly suffering from memory loss, muscle and joint pain, intestinal and heart problems, fatigue, rashes, sores, and running noses as a result of their service in the Gulf

War. . . . Physicians have been unable to diagnose or treat the cause of the disorders. Despite the Department of Defense's position that no evidence exists for exposure to chemical warfare agents during the Gulf War, this investigation indicates that there is substantial evidence supporting claims that U.S. servicemen and women were exposed to low level chemical warfare agents and possibly biological toxins." The report then raised an issue that still remains a focal point of current research and controversy: "Little is known about the long-term consequences of exposure to low levels of nerve gas, although most are known to have cumulative toxic effects. Even less is known about complications which might arise from exposure to combined agents and combined agent weapons. Non-lethal exposure to pesticides can result in memory loss, and nerve agents are chemically related to pesticides."

The document, which called for intensive research into low-level exposure to these toxins, was written by James J. Tuite III, then a doctoral candidate in political science at Catholic University who had joined Riegle's committee staff a few months before as a university fellow. His first major task came randomly: Riegle's home office in Michigan had received a series of complaining letters from Gulf War veterans, and it fell to Tuite, as the new guy, to find out what was going on. The stocky, balding Tuite, then forty-three years old, had some unanticipated assets: He was a hard-nosed former Secret Service agent whose last assignment had been as the forensic science research coordinator in the agency's laboratory division. Earlier, in the 1980s, he had served on the Middle East desk in the Secret Service intelligence division.

Tuite interviewed GIs and heard stories about chemical alarms constantly going off, preceded, in some cases, by loud explosions and strange smells. The physical difficulties would begin two or three days later. The Senate aide suspected chemical fallout as the essential cause of Gulf War syndrome, but—like a good cop—he investigated other possibilities and found there were many. The published report, as drafted by Tuite, noted that there were "other possible causes" for the illnesses, "such as the use of investigational anti–nerve agent drugs (PB), exposure to pesticides, petrochemicals, burning landfills and oil wells, depleted uranium from anti-tank munitions, or exposure to other environmental hazards . . . Each of these possible causes of unexplained illness should be systematically researched." It took years for the federal government to begin researching the questions posed by Tuite. As of this writing, there are no answers.

IN AN INTERVIEW, Tuite described himself as being innocent about the ways of Washington bureaucracy at the time of the report's publication on September 9, 1993. He thought he had made an important connection between the sick GIs and the possibility of low-level chemical warfare poisoning. "I never expected the response," he told me. "It was like World War III"—and he became a target.

A few days before the report was published, Tuite was telephoned by a Pentagon lieutenant colonel, who told him that she had discussed the issue of chemical fallout with "the chairman"—Colin Powell's retirement would not take place for three more weeks—and, so she claimed, Powell had "assured" her that there had been no fallout. This exchange then took place, Tuite said:

"You can't release the report."

"Why not?"

"Because it's classified."

There were powerful forces, Tuite thought, that did not want his report published.

Powell's assurances that there had been no chemical warfare poisoning quickly passed through the chain of command. A few days after that phone call, Tuite was told that Air Force Lieutenant General James R. Clapper, director of the Defense Intelligence Agency, had seen Powell early in the morning of September 9 and then told a weekly meeting of his senior staff that Riegle's report could not be correct. Clapper allegedly had said that Iraq had not used chemical weapons in the Gulf War and had not deployed chemical weapons near the Kuwaiti theater of operations.

Tuite realized that he was embroiled in a political war and soon came to believe that the Pentagon was not interested in the truth. Colin Powell and his fellow generals considered the report to be "a major blemish on what is perceived as the brightest military moment in the last fifty years," Tuite told me. "They'll do anything to protect it."

General Clapper, who retired in 1995, explained in a subsequent interview that there was a benign reason for the Pentagon's reaction to the Riegle report: a widespread belief that no chemical weapons had been used in Iraq and that Iraq had not deployed chemical weapons near the war zone. Clapper said that he might well have discussed the report with General Powell—though he had no memory of doing so, he said—and most certainly would have relayed his disregard for the Riegle report to his senior staff. "At the time," Clapper said, "I didn't find it credible."

Over the next few years, Clapper added, he would begin to change his mind as more information became available and more service personnel became ill. He began wondering about PB pills and the impact of the desert environment on the soldiers. When he first learned of the Riegle report, Clapper insisted, he had no reason to suspect that chemical fallout had any connection to the illnesses.

As the debate over the military cover-up intensified, desperately sick American veterans, vitalized by publicity over the Riegle report, were beginning to show up in far greater numbers at VA hospitals across America, seeking help. Jim Tuite and Don Riegle were overwhelmed with telephone calls and E-mail, many from men and women still on active duty who said they were sick but were afraid to tell their superiors. Gulf War veterans' groups began to organize, as Vietnam veterans had done a generation earlier. The American Legion and disabled veterans' groups began to lobby Congress for additional benefits on behalf of the sick Gulf War GIs. The number of needy veterans on file at the VA, which had set up a registry in 1992 for those believing they had become ill in the Gulf War, rose from three thousand in September to eleven thousand by the end of the year.

The Pentagon continued to insist that there had been no chemical fallout in the Gulf, and most of the veterans flocking to VA hospitals were still being told that they were victims of stress. Many others, even those awarded benefits, were officially depicted in VA records as being afflicted with specific illnesses, such as arthritis, that—as the GIs sensed—were merely symptoms of something more widespread.

The battle lines had been drawn.

7

Bureaucracy

SARA LISTER HAD been out of the game for fourteen years when she arrived at the Pentagon in the spring of 1994 as the army's assistant secretary for manpower and reserve affairs. A Democratic lawyer, she had served as general counsel for the army in the Carter administration and then became general counsel of Washington's transit authority, overseers of the city's new high-tech subway system.

Finding a solution for Gulf War syndrome was one of her responsibilities, and Lister quickly learned, she told me, she was in a no-win situation. The issues were no longer medical but political, and the key decisions were being made by the office of the secretary of defense. "In terms of the bureaucracy," Lister explained in an interview, "that meant that the folks who care the most—the services—were only indirectly involved. It was run by the Pentagon's office of health affairs." It was her belief, Lister said, as the army official in charge of manpower affairs, that "the veterans should be taken care of." It didn't happen.

"It's a case study," Lister added, "of how the system is going to get screwed up," with the suffering Gulf War veterans being victimized once again. "They fell between a rock and a hard place. The Defense Department is so difficult—all reactive mode. Nobody can do positive stuff. It's the world's most difficult bureaucracy."

The Pentagon's leadership, buffeted by Riegle's report, was in full denial. In May 1994, General John M. Shalikashvili, the new chairman of the Joint Chiefs of Staff, and William J. Perry, the secretary of defense, signed a joint letter to all veterans assuring them that, despite what they were reading and hearing in the media, "there is no information, classified or unclassified, that indicates that chemical or biological weapons were used in the Persian Gulf." The letter went on to assure the veterans that they were welcome at any military or VA hospital and would be "given a full medical evaluation and any medical care that you need." There was a catch, as Lister knew: William Perry and his deputy, John M. Deutch, former chairman of the MIT chemistry department and an expert on chemical warfare, remained convinced— along with Dr. Stephen C. Joseph, the assistant secretary of defense for health affairs—that Gulf War syndrome was the result of stress. A Pentagon survey, ordered by Joseph, reached thousands of GIs and found no clinical evidence for a single unique illness or syndrome among the Gulf veterans. There was no smoking gun, and thus they concluded the syndrome had to be driven by emotions and psychology.

Meanwhile, sick Gulf War veterans were reporting to the VA by the thousands with complaints that had nothing to do with possible exposure to chemical or biological warfare agents. Many of them were in supply and administrative units and had not seen combat, nor had they been stationed near the Kuwaiti theater of operations. A newly energized Congress was beginning to raise troublesome questions about other, lesser known, medical dangers in the Gulf War and the military's handling of them. For example, a 1994 report by the Senate Committee on Veterans' Affairs was devastating in its criticism of the Pentagon's handling of the experimental drug PB. Despite its promises to the FDA, not only did the military give GIs no warning about its dangerous side effects, they mandated that the drug be taken by all soldiers in the Persian Gulf, even in cases where individuals had an adverse response. The Senate committee further learned that PB was effective against only one nerve agent, soman, and only if followed by two other medicines. Yet, the committee noted in its report, the Pentagon "had no reason to believe that the Iraqis were more likely to use soman" than another, less persistent, nerve agent known as sarin, which was also in the Iraqi arsenal. Most significantly, the Senate reported, there was research indicating that PB, when combined with any exposure to pesticides and insect repellents—which were in wide use in the fly-ridden desert—became as much as seven times as toxic as when taken alone. There was a synergistic effect: GIs who took PB became more vulnerable to pesticides, and those exposed to pesticides became more vulnerable to PB. "This could explain," the Senate committee said in its report, "the serious neurological symptoms experienced by many Gulf War veterans."

Senator Riegle published another report in the fall of 1994, also drafted by Jim Tuite, that focused anew on the links between American exports of military equipment to Iraq and the Gulf War illnesses. The veterans' medical problems were becoming more widespread, the report noted: "Many of the signs and symptoms of illnesses initially experienced by the veterans of the Persian Gulf War are now being experienced by their spouses and families. This data confirms that these illnesses are becoming a major threat to the health and well-being of a significant and rapidly growing number of individuals." Two other congressional committees subsequently reported a significant number of birth defects and illnesses in the families of Gulf War veterans. In one typical account, Nancy Kapplan of Southington, Connecticut, a registered nurse who was married to an army helicopter pilot, told a House subcommittee in 1996 that medical issues "have plagued our lives since the day I opened my husband's duffel bag" and handled "his wet, soiled clothing" upon his return from the Gulf. Within three weeks, Mrs. Kapplan added, she and her two sons were diagnosed with asthma, and one of her daughters was hospitalized for six weeks with toxic shock, gangrene, and necrotizing fascitis "after I stored my husband's bags in her room."

Other studies by Congress and veterans' groups raised questions about the possibility of widespread radiation poisoning from American use in the Gulf of depleted-uranium (DU) shells and bombs, the first such use in military history. DU, little understood outside the military, is a highly toxic heavy-metal by-product of the uranium-enrichment process for producing weapons-grade nuclear material. DU is about 60 percent as radioactive as naturally occurring uranium ore, and has a half-life—that is, remains toxic—for 4.5 billion years. DU is cheap, is extremely dense, ignites spontaneously, and can pierce even the heaviest of armor with ease. DU artillery shells and bombs became the weapon of choice for the U.S. military in the late 1980s; shells and bombs containing more than 600,000 pounds of DU were flung at Iraqi tanks and troops in the Gulf War, contaminating much of the battlefield. One army training manual, published by the Chemical Corps, noted that a DU artillery shell, upon striking a tank, would aerosolize into the turret, ensuring that crew members "will inhale large amounts of DU dust." Soldiers and noncombatants "moving in, on, or near such vehicles after such an accident," added the manual, "should be considered contaminated." Despite such explicit data, the Pentagon was insisting in the early and mid-1990s that there was no evidence linking the use of DU munitions to Gulf War syndrome. Those who tried to raise the issue were rebuffed. Dr. Asaf Durakovic, a medical unit commander in the Gulf War, discovered acute radiation poisoning among a group of soldiers who, in the days after the war, had worked on battle-damaged tanks and vehicles. Dr. Durakovic later told a House subcommittee that tests showed that fourteen of the GIs were contaminated. While working after the war as chief of nuclear medicine at a VA medical center in Wilmington, Delaware, he sought to conduct follow-up studies. "I was ridiculed," Dr. Durakovic told Congress. There was "total lack of interest on the part of the VA to do anything for those unfortunate patients. I received phone calls from DOD [the Department of Defense] suggesting that this work is not going to yield meaningful information and should be discontinued." Durakovic was later terminated by the VA.

SHORTLY AFTER HER arrival in the Pentagon, Sara Lister told me, she began to learn more about stress. There was a high-level briefing on Gulf War syndrome given by the Army Surgeon General at which a senior military doctor explained that many factors were at work in making the GIs sick, "but a lot of it was stress." The Marine Corps was much more blunt, Lister added, putting out "the line that people who get Gulf War illnesses are weaker." Other factors were at work to diminish the possibility of doing more for the veterans:

- The army's Judge Advocate Corps raised questions about the possible legal issues that would arise if the military assumed responsibility for the Gulf War victims.
- There were the usual budget issues, as the army was being forced by the secretary of defense and the White House to cut spending wherever possible. "We were fighting for every penny we could get," Lister said.
- And there was the sad fact that the men and women who do the fighting and get the illnesses were never a priority in the turf fights that dominate so much of day-to-day life in the Pentagon. "The senior officers are too caught up in politics, and there's not enough caring about the troops," Lister said. "Too many generals have forgotten what it's like to be soldiers."

In retrospect, Lister said, the critical mistake that she and the senior generals made revolved around the acceptance of stress in explaining away Gulf War syndrome. Stress obviously was a factor in the illnesses, Lister said. But, she added, "*stress* is a dirty word for veterans. We should have figured out another word" and understood that "the illness could well have multiple causes." She and others on her staff—

including some generals—realized, Lister added, that "there were as many causes of Gulf War syndrome as there are human beings."

That knowledge did not change policy. In 1995 General Ronald Griffith, the former commander of the Third Armored Division, was appointed the army's vice chief of staff. He understood, as did Lister, that there was much more than stress behind Gulf War syndrome. "I was convinced," Griffith told me, "that the people who are sick are sick from the environment" in the desert. "It was the nastiest environment I'd ever seen." His troops had arrived in-country in late 1990 at the huge al-Jubayl port in Saudi Arabia and were briefly bivouacked a few miles away, pending further assignment. He and his aides called their camp Andersonville, Griffith related, after the brutal Civil War prison in Georgia. The area was polluted with smoke, diesel fuel, and insecticides. Conditions in the Gulf remained foul throughout the war, Griffith added, and those Pentagon officials who were insisting that Gulf War syndrome was caused exclusively by stress had made a huge mistake, in his view.

But, Griffith added, he also shared the belief of those same Pentagon officials that illness affecting the Gulf veterans had nothing to do with Iraqi chemical or biological warfare agents. There was no cover-up, Griffith told me, because there was nothing to cover up.

To say, as Griffith could in the mid-1990s, that there was a solid basis for the Gulf War syndrome would only buttress those outsiders, in the Congress and the veterans' groups, who were insisting that the Pentagon knew more than it was acknowledging about fallout from the bombing of Iraqi chemical depots. Griffith's dilemma was acute: He wanted nothing more than to take care of his soldiers, as a good officer would, but he was the army's second-highest officer in a government that was insisting that service in the Gulf War had nothing to do with America's sick GIs.

The general did what was prudent—and said nothing.

8

Enter Hillary Clinton (Briefly)

THE ISSUE OF who was sick and why was a hot political issue by early 1995, with the potential to get ugly. Gulf
War veterans were finally having success where it mattered—
in Congress and in the media. The Pentagon's insistence that
its sick soldiers were merely suffering from stress was creating
tension and a growing rift between the men and women
running the military and the men and women serving in it.
Saddam Hussein was continuing to resist the United Nations
requirement for unfettered access to his chemical and biological facilities, and American troops were constantly being
alerted for redeployment to the Gulf. Would they be safe?

It is not known what sparked the First Lady's interest.
Sometime after taking office, Stephen Joseph recalled in an
interview for this book, he and John Deutch were summoned to the White House for a briefing with Mrs. Clinton,
slides in hand and background papers at the ready. Deutch
told the excited young assistant secretary to stay in the background; he would handle the brief. It didn't turn out that
way, Joseph recalled. The First Lady was as crisp and to the

point as advertised. "I don't want you to confuse me with a lot of facts," she told Deutch, according to Joseph. "Just tell me why the Pentagon can't lead on this."

Hillary Clinton's initial interest seemed to be heartfelt. She, like many in Washington, wanted to know why the veterans were sick and what the government could do about it. She had met several times with Diana M. Zuckerman, a Yale-trained psychologist who had prepared a devastating report on PB for the Senate Committee on Veterans' Affairs; Zuckerman would later serve briefly on the White House staff. The First Lady's involvement was carefully measured, for it came at her lowest point in popularity; she was reviled for being too assertive, in the view of her critics, and was publicly called a "bitch" by the mother of House Speaker Newt Gingrich.

Nonetheless, Mrs. Clinton authorized Zuckerman to arrange two meetings with Gulf War syndrome victims at military hospitals near Washington, and listened, surrounded by her usual coterie of press, Zuckerman said, as the veterans told "heartrending stories about how sick they were." They also told the president's wife "how stinking the VA was. It was pretty shocking," Zuckerman added, "to have vets tell the First Lady how they were being treated." The Washington press corps couldn't have cared less. No significant newspaper stories appeared: the *Washington Post* ran a six-sentence item in its daily gossip column and a photograph of Mrs. Clinton at the hospital captioned, "Hillary making the rounds."

The First Lady's involvement remained in the background but was cited by Bill Clinton as a factor in his decision in May 1996 to appoint a presidential advisory committee to study Gulf War syndrome. Clinton urged the committee members to "leave no stone unturned" as it sought answers. The group, composed of twelve independent citizens, half of them in the medical field, held eighteen hearings over the summer and fall of 1996 and was asked by the president to continue its work through much of 1997.

ONE OF THE committee's senior investigators, James C. Turner, did the groundwork that produced the most dramatic disclosure of the Gulf War syndrome crisis: The American intelligence community had known since 1986 that nerve gas weapons were stored in the Iraqi weapons depot at Khamisiyah. That information, found in CIA files, was somehow not conveyed to the military units involved before the complex was destroyed in March of 1991, a few days after the end of the Gulf War. Studies eventually determined that upward of a hundred thousand American soldiers were in the path of the huge clouds of smoke—and nerve agent, presumably—that were generated.

The Pentagon's oft-stated assertion that no Americans had been exposed to chemical or biological agents was in tatters; so was the reputation of the Pentagon. The operative word in Washington was *cover-up*. "It was a damage-control operation from the outset," said Jim Turner of the Pentagon's approach, "but this [Khamisiyah] was taken to the nth degree. Nothing was going to be allowed to soil the great victory." After joining the committee, Turner had studied the many UNSCOM reports on its findings in Iraq, and eventually uncovered a Reuters press report, filed in February 1992 and published as a routine item in many American newspapers, about the destruction of the Khamisiyah depot. The report was also reprinted in the Pentagon's daily summary of significant newspaper and television reports in the previous twenty-four hours, which is made available to the press room and most offices in the building. Incredibly, no one in the Pentagon had connected the published report with the many complaints—which were widely known by early 1992—of Gulf War syndrome. "I began pushing on this," Turner explained in an interview. He was told in the spring of 1996 that "there was an incident they were concerned about." The Pentagon put out the bad news a few weeks later.

Many in Congress and the veterans' groups saw the cover-up of the Khamisiyah intelligence as confirmation of their belief that the veterans were sick primarily because they had been exposed to Iraqi nerve gas. The cover-up also proved to them that the Pentagon's Dr. Joseph had been lying all along, and his insistence on the importance of "stress"—a word that had become a magnet for distrust—was the major element in the lie.

All of the available evidence shows, however, that the intelligence failures at Khamisiyah were simply not known at the top until Jim Turner began asking questions. None of those interviewed for this book, including senior army officials such as Sara Lister and Ron Griffith, said they had any knowledge of the blunder until shortly before it was made public. There is a strong possibility, of course, that the CIA's failure in early 1991 to relay the information in time—which could have led to thousands of deaths—would never have been unraveled without Turner's intervention. That failure was a criminally negligent mistake, but it was not a cover-up.

Bill Arkin, in his research into the Gulf War, uncovered a more innocent—but just as mind-boggling—reason for the mass confusion inside the American intelligence community about Khamisiyah: The important arms depot had three different names inside the bureaucracy, and only the National Security Agency, responsible for communications intercepts, called it Khamisiyah. Internal army intelligence reports, Arkin said, referred to the weapons depot as Suq al Shuyukh, for a nearby town and bridge, and the official Defense Intelligence Agency database labeled the site as Tall al Lahm, for another nearby village. "It took four more years," Arkin added, "before all the connections were made."

Sara Lister recalled in an interview that she suffered through another widely reported dispute involving the alleged destruction of military logs dealing with reports of chemical and biological incidents in the Gulf War. Those logs were destroyed after the war, in violation of standing army orders, she said, because of gross negligence and incompetence on the part of its computer experts. An internal Army investigation eventually concluded that there was no criminal intent behind the loss of the logs, but many veterans told me early in 1998 that they remain convinced the documents were done away with to hide evidence of nerve gas exposure. I was specifically informed by congressional investigators and a number of veterans that an army reserve staff sergeant named Charley Fails of Jacksonville, Florida, had destroyed the chemical and biological logs in late 1996, just as the Khamisiyah affair became known. Fails, who was in charge of an army medical unit during the Gulf War, was said to have been ordered by an army major general to get rid of the documents and was now "too frightened" to talk.

Fails, who currently works in a gun shop, was anything but frightened when I saw him. He most certainly had shredded the chemical and biological logs in late 1996, he said, after his reserve medical unit was disbanded as part of an across-the-board army cutback. "I was told by the sergeant major to get rid of everything," Fails told me. "I didn't want to do it—it was part of my life." But an order was an order, and "I ripped it up, page by page."

Fails said there was nothing in the logs that suggested any prior knowledge of Iraqi nerve agents in Khamisiyah. "The people who blew up the dump didn't know what was in there." Fails said he had his own candidate for the causative agent behind the Gulf War syndrome: the PB pills. "I could not honorably give authorization for PB for my troops," Fails told me. "I questioned the side effects—dizziness, nose running, sweating. The same symptoms for a nerve gas attack. How can you tell if your troops have been hit with a nerve agent attack if you've already given them one?"

Charley Fails's lingering questions about what isn't known about the possible dangers of PB may be more relevant to the Gulf War syndrome issue than a congressional witch hunt for Pentagon liars. Even Jim Turner, the harshest critic of the Pentagon's intelligence failure at Khamisiyah, acknowledged that there are no answers—yet—to the important question of what ails the Gulf War GIs. "God knows what we blew up" at Khamisiyah and at dozens of other Iraqi depots after the war, Turner said. "My take is that the experts are going to be arguing about cause for the next fifty years. The answer is to take care of the vets. We're still not doing it."

Unfortunately, the final report of the presidential advisory committee also did not do it. In one of its last meetings, the twelve committee members agreed that the published report should recommend that the government's investigation of Gulf War syndrome be transferred away from the Pentagon to another agency because of the Pentagon's loss of credibility over Khamisiyah. The final report did not include that strong recommendation, but it was exceedingly critical nonetheless of the Pentagon for its sloppiness in record keeping over the distribution of vaccines and PB pills during the war. It urged, as such committee reports invariably do, more long-term studies into the effects of depleted-uranium and nerve gas poisoning. Most significantly, the committee seemed to side with the veterans by noting that Pentagon doctrine had never considered the possibility that low-level exposure to nerve gas could eventually lead to chronic illness. It recommended that the military contract with outside groups for an independent study to determine whether there had been any such exposure during the Gulf War. The Pentagon had been categorical during the Gulf War syndrome dispute in insisting that there was no medical basis for assuming the possibility of chronic illnesses among, as Stephen Joseph repeatedly said to Congress, "persons exposed to low levels of chemical nerve agents who did not first exhibit acute symptoms of toxicity." In essence, Joseph's position was that if a soldier was not killed or immediately incapacitated by the nerve gas, he would not subsequently become ill.

Despite its many progressive recommendations, the presidential committee undermined its credibility in the eyes of Congress and the Gulf War veterans by supporting the contention of Joseph and his superiors at the Pentagon that stress was the key factor in Gulf War syndrome. "Although some veterans clearly have service-connected illnesses," the report said, "current scientific evidence does not support a causal link between the symptoms and illnesses reported today." The one such link was stress, the report added, which "manifests in diverse ways, and is likely to be an important contributing factor to the broad range of physiological and psychological illnesses currently being reported by Gulf War veterans." The committee ignoring ongoing epidemiological research in medical schools and laboratories across the nation, also specifically ruled out any known link between the illnesses and such environmental risks as chemical warfare agents and PB.

In subsequent months, some members of the committee made it known that they eventually came to have serious doubts about the report that was issued in their name. "We said clearly that stress was a factor, a neglected factor and even a contributing factor," advisory committee member Arthur L. Caplan said in an interview, "but stress is not a sufficient reason [for Gulf War syndrome] and not the single reason. The single-bullet theory just doesn't hang together." Caplan, a professor at the Center for Bioethics at the University of Pennsylvania, added that he and other committee members were stunned early in 1998 when Dr. Joyce C. Lashof, the University of California professor who chaired the committee, suddenly "began pushing the stress causation button very hard" in press interviews and television appearances—in effect, parroting the Stephen Joseph approach. At that point, Caplan told me, he and other committee members began to distance themselves from the committee report. By his count, Caplan said, as many as six members of the committee ended up feeling that the final report minimized their belief that nerve gas exposure—triggered by American bombing and demolition—may be a contributing factor to the syndrome.

"Getting into stress drove everyone crazy," Caplan added. "The vets think stress means they're nuts. Congress thinks stress means cowards. And scientists think stress means immunology. We were right to get stress as a possible contributing factor. That said, I believe the witch hunt for a single cause is a lot of nonsense. It provides a way for Congress, the Pentagon, and you and me to avoid paying the freight for illness that resulted in service in the Gulf.

"Why don't we just settle accounts with these guys [the veterans]? Let's just pay the kids and get them well."

Caplan has been fearless in making his point of view public, telling a House Subcommittee on Veterans' Affairs hearing in February 1998 that he found the Pentagon's—and the advisory committee's—citing of stress as a major contributing factor to Gulf War syndrome to be "absurd and at times offensive . . . The identification of stress has led some to conclude that our committee felt that Gulf War illness is all in the minds of veterans, that some veterans must be making up their symptoms or that only those too weak or frail or unfit for service would succumb to the psychological impact of deployment in an alien environment and exposure to combat fought with terrible technological weapons."

What went wrong in the committee? Caplan, asked that question in an interview, blamed the committee's ground rules, which limited the investigation to government data. One advisory committee investigator, Jonathan C. Tucker, was abruptly fired for going outside official channels to collect data. Tucker, who now directs the chemical and biological warfare studies program at the Center for Nonproliferation Studies in Monterey, California, said that he made the mistake "of taking the president's mandate to leave no stone unturned seriously." When he was fired, Tucker was given one hour to leave the advisory committee's offices.

Diana Zuckerman, who was brought into the White House by Hillary Clinton, spent a miserable year in the Science Office, waiting for a call—which never came—from the presidential advisory committee. She remains an admirer of the First Lady, she said, but watched sadly as the White House constantly seemed to defer to political necessities—and the Pentagon. At the time, the wildly popular Colin Powell was rumored to be a candidate for the Republican nomination for the presidency in 1996, and Clinton's aides "made it absolutely clear that we couldn't blame the earlier administration" for Gulf War syndrome. There also was a general reluctance to take on the Pentagon, Zuckerman said. "There was a strong mentality [that] if there were any technical and scientific decisions to be made they were to be made at the department level and not at the White House. It was idiotic." It was that same sense of caution, she added, that kept the presidential advisory committee—which had been sought so avidly by Hillary Clinton—from deciding not to communicate with whistle-blowers and others inside the government "who had information that was not consistent with the official position."

Jim Tuite, who drafted Don Riegle's early reports on Gulf War syndrome, views the advisory committee's failure to resolve any of the health issues in dispute as a failure of presidential leadership. Tuite said he was in a position to closely monitor the investigation, and he became convinced that the committee was closely tied to a White House that, in his view, is unable to stand up to the Pentagon. President Clinton and his wife, he said, "were trying to show care and concern" about an important issue involving the health of American soldiers but were not willing to pay the political price of a full-scale inquiry. The president, added Tuite, has been "afraid to take on the Pentagon" since his defeat over gays in early 1993. "Getting the First Lady involved demonstrates that he was not willing to do anything"—as Clinton had publicly promised the Gulf War veterans—to get to the truth. "Hillary was involved," Tuite said, "and went to a few hospitals. And then all of a sudden she dropped out."

Forming a committee "is a time-honored delaying tactic," Tuite added. "Study what you already know, and call for more studies. Keep on setting up panels."

In a subsequent interview, Don Riegle, who left the Senate in 1994, expressed disgust with President Clinton over his reluctance to get personally involved in the issue. "He's the commander in chief and he's in a position to force some accountability, but there doesn't seem to be the stomach to challenge the Pentagon.

"Where's his conscience?"

9

Stephen Joseph

STEPHEN C. JOSEPH emerged as the Darth Vader of the Gulf War veterans' movement, in the eyes of the GIs and their congressional supporters, a Pentagon apparatchik who gave a patina of professionalism and a vague medical phrase—"stress"—to the military's insistence that the ailing veterans were malingering cowards. Joseph, who resigned as assistant secretary for health affairs in early 1997, doesn't buy it. He says he has no regrets and "would do it again." The doctor, who began his career as a pediatrician, is convinced that the ailing veterans and the American people lost an important opportunity amid the squabbling to come to terms with one of the unspoken and unseen consequences of the Gulf War and all other wars: psychological impairment.

"There is a very tight connection between physical symptoms and psychological factors," Joseph said in a long, reflective interview about his three years at the Pentagon. "This is a fact of life we all understand. But we put it aside in a military context. We all had a neighbor who came back from one or another war and sat on the porch, staring at nothing, for six months. But we don't—we can't come out and talk about it openly. It was like being in a 1940s war movie in which nobody ever got hurt. What combat can do to people's psyche is still an unspoken, immutable issue.

"The Gulf War syndrome offered us the opportunity to mature and to acknowledge," Joseph added. "But nobody could do it—not the vets, not us. When I'd say 'stress' in a congressional hearing, the congressional windbags would ask, 'Are you saying it's all in their head?' and the vets would all jump up."

Joseph, who today operates a health management consulting practice in Santa Fe, New Mexico, is still convinced, he said, that the various Gulf War ailments are "a combination of the physical and the psychological, with the driving force being psychological. That's the tragedy of the whole thing. It's my job to make people's health better, and we've not done it in this case. It would be ten times better for the veterans of the next war if we can get them to understand the issue of combat stress. The veterans weren't able to handle the message, and they bear some of the responsibility, too."

Bearded and intense, the type A Joseph was no newcomer to high-profile tension when he came to Washington. He served four years in the 1980s dealing with the AIDS epidemic and the politics of New York City as that city's health commissioner. He became the Pentagon's top "doc"—the military's usual sobriquet for physicians—in late 1993, a few months after the Riegle report had come out. There was a crunch of other issues: medical units throughout the armed forces were being consolidated and eliminated under the tightened defense budget; the final Agent Orange settlement was still being worked out; and there were new revelations about the casualties of America's early studies of radiation poisoning.

Joseph knew little, he said, about Gulf War syndrome, but his first meeting with John Deutch, the deputy defense secretary who was his immediate superior, led to this question: "How are we going to deal with Gulf War syndrome?" Deutch's conclusion, Joseph recalled, was that the "best thing" would be for the issue to disappear, "but it was clear to Deutch that it wasn't going to go away."

His approach, Joseph said, was to begin surveying Gulf War veterans one by one, and in depth, in an attempt to get a definition of the illness. "I was trying to learn, through them," he said, "what was going on." Not everyone in the Pentagon thought Joseph's questionnaire made sense. Sara Lister told me that one of her military aides reported, after filling out the questionnaire, that it asked intrusive questions about drug use, drinking, and sexual practices—"things that would make people not tell you the truth. Joseph," Lister added, "did not understand soldiers."

Nonetheless, twenty thousand interviews later, a joint Pentagon and VA research team came to the conclusion in early 1996, Joseph said, that there was "no single bullet—no overriding issue" that stretched across the various illnesses. "There was no mystery illness. There was no Gulf War illness. We didn't have a case definition and couldn't say if this ailment is or isn't Gulf War syndrome." The one factor that seemed most closely associated with all of the cases, Joseph added, was psychological stress. The Pentagon doctor would repeatedly cite this study until he left office the next year.

Congress and the veterans, he knew, had already made clear their objections to the concept of stress, as more and more veterans, citing varied symptoms, continued to register with the VA. In one highly publicized case, a fifteen-year veteran of the air force named Michael Donnelly fell ill in 1995 with a fatal case of amyotrophic lateral sclerosis, also known as Lou Gehrig's disease, after being exposed at home to malathion, an insect spray whose chemical makeup is similar to, though much weaker than, nerve agent. The attractive Donnelly, of South Windsor, Connecticut, had flown forty-four combat missions during the war, often through heavy smoke, without ever being warned of the threat from chemical or biological exposure. He now saw himself, he told a congressional hearing, as "yet another veteran from the Gulf War with a chronic illness." The VA, echoing Joseph's findings, told him that there was no link between his illness and his service in the Gulf War. Donnelly dramatically told Congress that it was too late to save his life and made the case for his fellow veterans, asking at the hearing why the Pentagon and VA weren't "warning everyone else who served in the Gulf that they may get sick in the future, just as I got sick four years after I returned from the Gulf. How many other people out there are waiting for that one exposure that's going to put them over the top?"

Such complaints, while moving, Joseph thought, were utter nonsense. "We know," he told me, "that Donnelly doesn't have Gulf War syndrome. I know I don't come across as warm and friendly," Joseph said. "It's not one of my strong points. But the fact is I do have a real empathy and sympathy for these guys, who periodically go out and save the country's butt. And I understand their confusion, anger, and sense of being cut off and let down. At the same time, reality is what reality is." Joseph never hesitated to tell Congress and the presidential advisory committee about stress and what he thought. There was a buzz saw of complaint, and Joseph and his questionnaire became the target of angry congressional ridicule.

In his interview with me, he returned the ridicule. "There's this wonderful American combination," the doctor said with bitterness. "Political hypocrites and hucksters in the administration, in Congress, media jackals and Dr. Frankenstein types—pseudoscientists—and soon the whole thing got swept away.

"It did such a disservice to the vets."

A NY RATIONAL CHANCE of winning his struggle with Congress over the importance of stress disappeared, Joseph told me, with the revelation of the intelligence snafu at Khamisiyah. "It all hit the fan then," Joseph said, "and all credibility was lost—mine and the Pentagon's." Joseph had nothing to do with Khamisiyah and yet, by sheer chance, he found himself scheduled to testify on Gulf War syndrome before Congress a few days after the Pentagon made its mistakes public. No one from the Defense Department joined him. "They were hanging me out to dry," Joseph told me. "My advisers kept on telling me that if they can't send a three-star [general] up there to testify with you, why go up there? I didn't feel I could walk away because it really was a medical issue." Joseph recalled his fury after a jarring encounter with Representative Christopher Shays, a Republican from Connecticut, who had emerged as a leading advocate for the ailing Gulf War veterans. Shays, chairman of the human resources subcommittee of the House Committee on Government Reform and Oversight, clearly suspected that the Pentagon's doctor had played a role in the Khamisiyah cover-up.

> *Shays:* When did you know there was a chemical weapon in any of these bunkers?
> *Joseph:* When did I know . . . ?
> *Shays:* Yes.
> *Joseph:* Several days before the press conference.
> *Shays:* How many days before?
> *Joseph:* I can't tell you, exactly.
> *Shays:* No, no, no. You can.
> *Joseph:* No. I can't tell you exactly, Mr. Chairman.
> *Shays:* Why can't you? This is a big issue . . . and you're telling me it's a forgettable event?
> *Shays:* That is not at all what I've said, Mr. Chairman.

BY THE END of 1996, Joseph, as the Pentagon's most visible defender in a losing struggle over responsibility for the Gulf War veterans, felt vulnerable. He was right. There was little public support or communication from John White, who had replaced John Deutch as deputy secretary of defense, or from any of the senior generals and admirals on the Joint Chiefs of Staff. William Perry, the secretary of defense, had remained aloof from the issue, shunting it to his deputies and to Joseph's office.

"I could see it coming," Joseph said. "I could see that John White was about to walk me off the plank." Joseph was convinced—he would not say on what basis—that Perry had not been told what he needed to know in advance about Khamisiyah and, in general, about the underlying medical issues in the crisis over Gulf War syndrome. The Khamisiyah debacle was especially troubling, given its disastrous impact on Joseph's ability to defend the Pentagon's position. It was always his belief, Joseph told me, that someone at a low level had seen the intelligence in time to prevent the demolition of that depot but decided, without checking further, "not to worry about it." Joseph said he eventually did learn that Khamisiyah had been suspected, before the Gulf War, of being a storage depot for chemical weapons, but a low-level analyst disputed that assessment, and it was routinely targeted for demolition. Joseph wasn't sure how much Defense Secretary William Perry, whom he admired greatly, knew about all this.

So Assistant Secretary of Defense Joseph did the unmentionable: He went outside the chain of command and asked for a meeting with the secretary. "My philosophy is," Joseph told me, "you do what you've got to do, and if it doesn't work—you're gone." He was prepared to resign. Perry, playing it by the book, invited John White to attend. As White listened, steely-eyed, Joseph told the defense secretary that he felt he was "being hung out to dry" by the Pentagon bureaucracy and had especially been poorly served over Khamisiyah. "I can't be sure," Joseph added, "that you're getting all the information from the intelligence and operational side [of the Pentagon] that you need."

He could see from Perry's response, Joseph said, that the defense secretary was nonplussed. "When I was done, he looked at White and asked, 'Is that so? Is it true that we don't have complete confidence that we know everything we need to know from intelligence and operations?' " White, speaking carefully, acknowledged that there were some problems, Joseph recalled. The tense meeting ended when Bill Perry "looked at me and said, 'I wish you wouldn't resign.' " He stayed on, Joseph said, until Perry left the Pentagon five months later. Perry did not respond to a request to be interviewed for this book. And John Deutch, praised by Joseph for his willingness not "to sweep the issue under the rug," similarly did not wish to extensively discuss the Pentagon's handling of Gulf War syndrome.

Deutch did say he had been introduced to the subject in late 1993 by the late Les Aspin, a former congressman who was secretary of defense (he was fired a few months later by Clinton). "I have an issue you've got to handle," Deutch quoted Aspin as telling him. "I don't want this to be another Agent Orange." Deutch, who is now back teaching chemistry at MIT, added dryly: "If ever there was a question of good intentions going bad, this was it. It's an example of how a government that wants to do right somehow cannot."

10

Nearing a Resolution

WITH JOSEPH'S DEPARTURE, much of the fight went out of the Pentagon. Stress was no longer the holy grail; it was now depicted as just another element in the complicated epidemiology of Gulf War syndrome. And, for the first time since the Gulf War ended in 1991, the American government said it would begin to directly treat the veterans' symptoms. It would try to get them well.

Much of this became known at a House oversight subcommittee hearing in February 1998, at the height of the Monica Lewinsky follies. The hearing attracted no press attention, but it made headlines for the veterans. The GIs' new heroes were the congressional odd couple of Representative Shays, the sometimes caustic Republican from Connecticut, and Representative Bernard Sanders, the idealistic independent from Vermont. For more than two years the two men had sponsored hearings, organized research, nurtured distraught veterans, and refused to accept the Pentagon's definition of stress.

The two congressmen saw the issue in moral terms, using the power of their public office—as President Clinton chose not to do—to intervene on behalf of the veterans. "Our oversight mission," Shays, chairman of the subcommittee, said at the opening of a hearing in March 1996, "is to stand watch over the process to make sure that nothing compromises our moral obligation to those who served. Not potential cost. Not missing medical records. Not bureaucratic inertia. Not the lack of a single theory of causation for diffuse symptoms." Sanders has similarly castigated the Pentagon and the VA for their treatment of the Gulf War veterans, and at one point dramatically called for a "Manhattan Project type of organization . . . to solve this problem."

Sometimes they were corny. Sometimes they spoke too much. Sometimes they were too conspiratorial. Sometimes they were dead wrong. In the end, they began to get their way.

ONCE AND FOR all, stress was buried as a governmental excuse for doing nothing by Dr. John Feussner, chief of research and development for the VA and chairperson of a government-wide coordinating group on medical aspects of Gulf War syndrome. Feussner told Shays and Sanders that he and his colleagues believed that "if we had some definitive treatments" for Gulf War syndrome, "we would become less concerned about cause because at least we could do something better for the patients. . . . But I do not believe that all of these various complaints fit neatly under one diagnosis of stress. I think that much of the research has shown that this is much more complicated than that and much more diverse than that. So I would be reluctant to blame stress as an explanation for all of this."

With those phrases, the American government sued for peace in its war over stress with its ninety thousand suffering veterans.

There was a second breakthrough, arising in response to a question from Bernie Sanders. "A couple of months ago," Sanders said to Feussner, "I was at a [Gulf War] veterans' meeting in Springfield, Vermont . . . and on Saturday, just this week, in Burlington. . . . In Springfield I said, 'Tell me about memory loss, short-term memory.' Everybody in the room started laughing, because almost without exception every one of these people—hardworking Vermonters—were suffering from memory loss. . . . We were talking about other problems that people have and guys were saying, 'You know I go into a supermarket and I walk past the detergent section—they have that funny smell from detergents. When I smell that, I get sick.' Then they were talking about scented candles, and they were all laughing about that. When they are around scented candles, they get sick. When their wives wear perfume, they get sick. In Burlington, in the meeting two days ago, we talked about short-term memory loss, and everybody in the room stood up. A guy who is in a car with his family, they are out on a vacation having a great time. Suddenly, he cannot remember the simplest things. Now, I have a hard time understanding how healthy people thirty-five to forty years old suffer from short-term memory loss."

Sanders finally asked Feussner, "I want you to tell me what you have learned. What treatment do we have? After seven years, is there any treatment?" Feussner's answer was straightforward: "I think Mr. Sanders's criticism on that is a fair criticism. At the moment, we have no active treatment trials ongoing in any of these areas. . . . [W]e have been fussing," the doctor explained, "over trying to come up with a case definition so we can study Persian Gulf veterans' illness, and we can't come up with a definition, so we don't generate treatment." Feussner added that he and his research colleagues were in the process of planning treatment trials, utilizing behavioral therapy and exercise therapy, for chronic fatigue and fibromyalgia, two illnesses, linked to multiple chemical sensitivity, that had struck many veterans.

A few moments later, Bernie Sanders recounted the experiences—as told in earlier testimony—of a physician who abated many of the veterans' symptoms by aggressively treating them with antibiotics. Feussner was initially skeptical: antibiotics are effective only against bacteria, and Gulf War syndrome is not triggered by any known bacterial disease. Sanders persisted, telling the VA doctor that "in Vermont, I specifically asked the guys who were hurting, 'Listen, no one can guarantee any cures. But if there were an experimental treatment that we are pretty sure was not going to make you worse than you are today, would you be prepared to undertake that?' Every hand in the room went up. Are you prepared," he asked Feussner, "to come to the state of Vermont and start this antibiotic therapy?" After a few moments of quibbling, the VA official finally said, "Yes. I will try to start an experimental trial of antibiotic therapies."

THERE WAS ONE more victory. After six years of insisting that there was no evidence linking the experimental drug PB to any Gulf War illness, Dr. Anna Johnson-Winegar, director of the Pentagon's biomedical and medical program, told the subcommittee that there "were no plans" to use PB in any future combat in the Gulf. The Pentagon, she added, would not ask the FDA for any further waivers.

The turnabout was astonishing, and Christopher Shays was gracious in acknowledging it. "I do want to say to you," he told the government physicians, "that I know there is enough blame to go around on the issue. Congress was asleep. I was asleep. We all were asleep on this issue. My big concern is the eagerness in which we try to undo the past and move forward."

A few weeks later, the VA formally adopted a rule that essentially did away with all previous rules, which gave veterans two years from the date of their service in the Gulf to file a claim for benefits. Under the new regulation, promulgated on March 6, 1998, veterans would have until the year 2001 to file claims for undiagnosed illness stemming from Gulf War duty. The deadlines had been eased in early 1997, but only on an interim basis.

THE GOVERNMENT'S RETREAT on the possibility of chemical exposures in the Gulf raises a chilling question: *What about the next time?*

Are there adequate defenses against chemical and biological warfare? For all of the Pentagon's talk in recent years about improved defenses, little has been done. The same chemical alarm systems that produced one misleading reading after another of imminent nerve gas attack in the Gulf War are still on duty, and still not capable of registering low levels of exposure. The GIs' gas masks and chemical protective suits have not been significantly improved, despite extensive—and still classified—Pentagon inquiries into their inadequacies. In an interview, Jim Tuite, who is still active in Gulf War veterans' affairs, accused the Pentagon of "defending our soldiers with Halloween masks and garbage bags."

There still is a morbid fear of biological warfare among military leaders, a fear—or fascination—that produces bizarre responses. When more than thirty-five thousand American GIs were mobilized once again in the Gulf in early 1998 for a showdown with Saddam Hussein that did not take place, the Clinton administration announced that the soldiers would all be provided with anthrax vaccine. The widely reported action drew a wry comment from Scooter Libby, who directed the Pentagon study of biological warfare before the 1991 invasion of Kuwait. "The good news is that our troops are vaccinated against anthrax," he told me. "The bad news is that he [Saddam Hussein] now knows what we're vaccinated against."

Finally, what about the responsibility of Generals Colin Powell and Norman Schwarzkopf? In their interviews with me, both men expressed support for their troops and dismay at the failure of the American government to provide unstinting medical care. "The first time I heard about Gulf War syndrome was through the press at the end of 1993," Schwarzkopf said. "I thought the Defense Department handled it very cavalierly. They blew these guys off.

"My God!" he added. "Anybody's who's sick deserves to be treated." Like Powell, Schwarzkopf also emphasized the fact that he retired in mid-1991 from the army. "The minute you are retired," the general told me, "you're cut off from the flow of events. When you leave, someone else is promoted, and the last thing they want is some old general coming back."

Those answers aren't good enough for the leaders of the Gulf War veterans' movement. "We've had no contact with Schwarzkopf and Colin Powell has been silent," said Paul Sullivan, executive director of the National Gulf War Research Center in Washington. "We sent Powell a letter asking to meet with him, and he said he had no time. We would welcome them home as fellow Gulf War veterans."

Retired Major General Don Edwards of the National Guard, who now works for Representative Bernie Sanders, believes that Powell's and Schwarzkopf's detachment reflects a widespread disconnect at the top of the officer corps. "It's almost like they had brain surgery," Edwards told me. "When they get to be three-star [lieutenant general] and above [full general], they seem to lose touch with the field troops and the reality that the important combat requirement is people. It's all about ego, self-success, and playing the game.

"How could true military leaders," he said of Powell and Schwarzkopf, "allow their soldiers to be treated the way these soldiers were treated?"

Former senator Don Riegle believes the two generals had "a precious obligation to protect those who fight the war before, during, *and* after. If they get sick in your war, I don't know how this concern can't take up most of every day. How about setting up a foundation? Do speeches? Set up a trust fund to help the vets? I'm not trying to be spiteful," Riegle added, "but how do you retire from your responsibility? If you lead people in battle, do you leave your own wounded? I've seen thousands of them, and these people were badly wounded."

Just what it was in the Persian Gulf air that had "badly wounded" the veterans remained unknown in mid-1998 and will remain so for years. Researchers have many candidates. The VA's Dr. William Baumzweiger has found high levels of lymphocytes in the spinal fluid of some GIs, and is convinced that they are suffering from chronic neurological problems. A Scottish research team headed by Dr. Goran A. Jamal of Glascow similarly determined that some victims of Gulf War syndrome were suffering from a measurable loss of central nervous system function. A Texas researcher, Dr. Robert W. Haley, found evidence of neurotoxic brain damage, most likely from exposure to low levels of chemical nerve agents, among the Gulf veterans he treated. A Georgetown University rheumatologist, Dr. Daniel J. Clauw, has reported evidence of chronic fatigue syndrome and multiple chemical sensitivity among the ailing soldiers. Clauw's findings echoed those of a study made public in 1997 by the VA that documented the extensive prevalence of chronic fatigue, multiple chemical sensitivity, and fibromyalgia among the veterans.

Any conclusive determination will await future research, and may never be possible. No air samples were taken during the war, and there is no way of re-creating the war's conditions. Most of the suffering Gulf War veterans are going about their lives, but they remain convinced that something was in the air during the war—a mystery disease that inflicted grievous harm.

Epilogue

The Last Battle

THE MILITARY'S RETREAT on Gulf War syndrome was not total. Eager to maintain an effective weapon, they have refused to reconsider their reliance on depleted-uranium (DU) shells and bombs, despite reports of serious contamination among allied soldiers and civilians living in the war zone in southern Iraq. The Pentagon's position is complicated by increasingly detailed evidence that the dangers of the radioactive materials were fully understood—and disregarded—by the army's weapons experts on the eve of the war.

The toll, unnoticed in the first years after the war, is steadily rising. At least thirty British soldiers who took part in the Gulf War have died of cancer, and veterans' groups in England have called for studies to determine whether radiation exposure from DU shells triggered the disease. In March of 1998, journalist Robert Fisk of the London *Independent* reported on what he termed a "chemical plague" that has afflicted thousands of Iraqi citizens who lived in or near the war zone. "The kidney problems, respiratory failures and cancers now being diagnosed among Allied veterans appear to be identical to those afflicting Iraqis," Fisk wrote, after touring hospitals in the area. "In most cases, the Iraqi victims were diagnosed only years later—just as Gulf War Syndrome was only grudgingly acknowledged in London and Washington, long after Allied troops had returned home." Fisk said he has learned that many former Iraqi soldiers have fallen and their doctors are blaming the DU shells. "Even now," the reporter noted, Saddam Hussein's regime has made not a single statement about the epidemic of cancer afflicting the largely Shiite Muslim population. Here, then, is something which President Clinton, Prime Minister [Tony] Blair [of Great Britain] and Saddam Hussein have in common: a total failure to explain the calamity afflicting thousands of their people after the 1991 conflict."

Ten days after Fisk's article appeared, John Donnelly, a Mideast correspondent for the San Jose *Mercury-News*, visited three hospitals in Iraq and reported a huge jump in the number of cancer cases in Basra, a city of 1.5 million residents in southern Iraq that was close to the war zone. Most alarming, doctors there told Donnelly, was a sharp rise in leukemia cases among the children, including some born more than nine months after the war. This suggests, Donnelly wrote, "that some environmental carcinogens may have lingered long after the war ended or that some war-related contaminants may be causing genetic damage." An Iraqi study found that the per capita rate of all cancers in southern Iraq was more than four times higher than in other regions to the north and west, and birth defects were nearly three times as high. The Iraqi government has said little publicly about the postwar surge in cancer cases, the reporter noted, presumably in fear of creating panic and unrest in the area surrounding Basra, where Saddam Hussein's troops suppressed a brief rebellion after the Gulf War. The citizens' anger seemed directed elsewhere. Donnelly quoted one mother as exclaiming, "We never had such numbers of diseases before the war. What pollution was in the bombs?"

The Iraqi war zone is still glowing with nuclear contamination, Donnelly added: "Measurement of radiation taken from destroyed Iraqi tanks in 1995, more than four years after the war, found readings eight times higher than normal background radiation."

The two newspaper articles attracted little attention in the United States. Neither did an equally grim study on the effects of DU that was made public in late February 1998 by a veterans'-rights group known as Swords to Plowshares. The 235-page report, utilizing data obtained under the Freedom of Information Act, concluded that American and British tanks and aircraft fired more than 630,000 pounds of radioactive DU weapons at Iraqi tanks during the war. The report, written by Dan Fahey, further estimated that "at least 400,000 veterans" could have been exposed to depleted uranium—a statistic, it must be noted, for which there was no direct evidence (which is undoubtedly why the major media has not written about it). But Fahey's report also included an array of devastating government documents showing that there is widespread awareness of the deleterious impact of DU. One memorandum, written a few days after the war by an army lieutenant colonel on duty at the Los Alamos National Laboratory, noted that there did exist a "relatively small amount of lethality data" for DU shells, and a continuing concern regarding the impact of DU on the environment. "[I]f no one makes a case for the effectiveness of DU on the battlefield," the colonel wrote, "DU rounds may become politically unacceptable and thus, be deleted from the arsenal." The officer suggested that, "to assure the future existence" of DU, "we should keep this sensitive issue at mind when after-action reports [on the Gulf War] are written." Other military records obtained by Fahey revealed that an army medical officer named Douglas L. Rokke recommended in the aftermath of the Gulf War that six damaged American tanks not be returned to the United States for repair because of high levels of radioactive contamination; the tanks were instead buried in the desert sand. The damaged tanks, Lieutenant Rokke added, "could not be placed on public display without substantial risk to health and safety of the public and members of the military." Radiological decontamination, he reported, "is not possible."

In an interview for this book, Rokke, now a captain in the army reserves, said that few soldiers during the war understood the risk from radioactive DU—but all do today. Rokke, who has a doctorate in physics, has become active in the Gulf War veterans' movement and is seeking VA compensation for radiological poisoning stemming from exposures in the war. The Gulf War veteran gave me copies of a series of cautionary after-action reports he and a team of medical corps colleagues produced on DU. "The team," Rokke wrote his superiors in 1993, "found that few unit personnel had any knowledge regarding the identification, actual hazards, decontamination, or retrograde of equipment involved in DU incidents or proper emergency medical procedures for treatment of individuals exposed to depleted uranium munitions." Rokke's unit also urged a major decontamination and cleanup for Kuwait "to salvage or dispose of depleted uranium contaminated equipment." Iraq was left on its own.

In his report for Swords to Plowshares, Dan Fahey noted that the radiation hazard posed by DU was widely recognized in the business world. In 1980, a New York State agency obtained a court order forcing a Pentagon arms supplier in Colonie to cease production of DU munitions because the plant was regularly exceeding a state limit of 150 microcuries per month for airborne emission of radioactivity. The 150 microcuries, Fahey wrote, correspond to a monthly release of less than one pound of uranium dust. The plant eventually was shut down and the building decontaminated. "[T]he amount of depleted uranium released in January and February, 1991, in Kuwait, Saudi Arabia and Iraq was more than 700,000 times greater than the amount that shut down the . . . plant," Fahey wrote.

Cleanup costs pose another headache. According to Fahey, the cost of safely removing some 150,000 pounds of depleted uranium—one fourth of that expended in the Gulf—at a military test site in Indiana is estimated at $4 billion to $5 billion. There are more than 1 billion pounds of excess depleted uranium in the United States, the residue of America's extensive nuclear weapons program, and the weapons producers give it away to firms that manufacture the very effective DU antitank shells and bombs.

The military attacked Fahey's report with heated criticism, some of it in language that was reminiscent of the Vietnam era. One senior Pentagon official raised questions about Fahey's patriotism, accusing the former navy officer, who was honorably discharged after the Gulf War as a conscientious objector, of having a personal political agenda—beyond the banning of DU—of "disarmament in general." Other criticism dwelled on the report's overwrought estimates of potential DU victims and ignored the substantial issues raised elsewhere—and backed up by documents obtained under the Freedom of Information Act. The attack on Fahey was all the more remarkable because it was led by Bernard Rostker, a special assistant to the deputy defense secretary, who replaced Stephen Joseph in early 1997 as the military's point man for Gulf War syndrome. Rostker's theoretical assignment, as announced by the Pentagon in the wake of the Khamisiyah disgrace, was to listen to the veterans and find ways "to build and maintain trust" in the American military. "It is vitally important for the Department to retain credibility with the veterans' community," Rostker said in his first annual report, issued in late 1997. "Reaching out and being responsive to the needs of our veterans is a very important part of our effort."

Instead, Rostker, an economist, has increasingly been seen by the veterans and their friends in Congress as a military spokesman who is prepared to double-talk—as they believe he has on depleted uranium—when it suits his purpose, or the purpose of the armed services. For example, Rostker was candid about the environmental dangers of DU in his annual report, which was made available to Congress and to veterans' groups. The Pentagon's "investigations into potential health hazards of depleted uranium point to serious deficiencies in what our troops understood about the health effects DU posed on the battlefields," Rostker wrote. "Combat troops or those carrying out support functions generally did not know that DU contaminated equipment, such as enemy vehicles struck by DU rounds, required special handling. . . .

The failure to properly disseminate such information to troops at all levels may have resulted in *thousands* of unnecessary exposures" (emphasis added).

However, in a tough-sounding speech to the American Legion in late March 1998, a few weeks after release of the Fahey report, Rostker minimized the environmental risks. He rhetorically asked whether it was safe to use DU munitions and then said: "The best answer is the actual exposure to depleted uranium is not medically significant. Let me be precise: to date DU exposure has not produced any medically detectable effects." His remarks inflamed some veterans. "Dr. Rostker is wrong," Doug Rokke said. "Some of us are sick. He should make a public apology."

Rostker added another rhetorical flourish in his American Legion speech. He declared that DU, which replaced tungsten carbide as the military's main antitank weapon, had been of lifesaving importance in the Gulf War—the implicit suggestion was that those who would deny DU to the troops were jeopardizing their well-being. DU artillery shells, he said, "undoubtedly saved thousands of American lives. Just ask any American tanker if he wants to face the Republican Guard in battle without every advantage we can provide."

Retired general Don Edwards, who commanded armored cavalry units while on active army duty, acknowledged that DU was a more efficient penetrator than shells made from tungsten. "You lose some effectiveness," Edwards told me, "but you don't lose a huge amount." On balance, he added, he would much prefer the use of tungsten: "It's more expensive, but it's obtainable, and it's so much safer for battlefield use that it's beyond belief."

Bill Arkin similarly concluded, after studying Iraqi tank

losses in the Gulf War, that the American reliance on DU weapons was overkill. "The truth is that the United States did not have any difficulty killing tanks," Arkin has written. The Soviet-designed Iraqi tanks "hardly seem the impregnable fortresses as once thought during the Cold War and DU rounds were hardly the centerpiece" of the American anti-tank arsenal. "Literally dozens of different types of non-DU anti-tank weapons slayed armored vehicles right and left. With even more capable smart weapons emerging, DU is no longer essential."

DU SHELLS AND bombs are now being offered for sale by the United States to foreign armies and air forces. Sales are brisk. American know-how, and radioactive poisoning, is being merchandised around the world.

It may not last.

The Gulf War veterans and their supporters in Congress have forced a resisting military and an intimidated White House to acknowledge that the price of war—even in smashing triumph—is high. Victory in the Gulf took a higher toll than first understood—as many as ninety thousand friendly-fire casualties and an environment perhaps despoiled by long-lasting radioactivity.

The lesson to be learned is this: Today's high-tech wars are too important and too dangerous to be left to the military, or to the politicians. Neither will risk all to protect their soldiers. Those men and women who do the fighting want their say, too, and are learning how to get it.

Further Readings

THE BEST MATERIAL on the epidemiology and politics of Gulf War syndrome can be found, not surprisingly, in published congressional hearings. See the hearings into "The Status of Efforts to Identify Persian Gulf War Syndrome" before the Subcommittee on Human Resources and Intergovernmental Relations of the House Committee on Government Reform and Oversight, chaired by Representative Christopher Shays (R-CT). The subcommittee's conclusions after nineteen months of hearings were published on November 7, 1997, and titled "Gulf War Veterans' Illnesses: VA, DoD Continue to Resist Strong Evidence Linking Toxic Causes to Chronic Health Effects." The Senate Committee on Veterans Affairs has held hearings into Gulf War syndrome since 1994. For early skepticism on the military use of pyridostigmine bromide, see "Is Military Research Hazardous to Veterans' Health? Lessons from World War II, the Persian Gulf, and Today," May 6, 1994. For the testimony of Generals Colin Powell and Norman Schwarzkopf, see the committee's hearings on January 9, January 29, and April 17,

1997, on "Persian Gulf War Illnesses." The cited Senate staff report, prepared by Diana Zuckerman, was published on December 8, 1994. The committee chairman is Senator Arlen Specter (R-PA). James Tuite's influential early reports on the Gulf War illnesses, prepared for the Senate Committee on Banking, Housing and Urban Affairs, are "The Gulf War Syndrome: The Case for Multiple Origin Mixed Chemical/Biotoxoin Warfare Related Disorders," published on September 9, 1993, and "U.S. Chemical and Biological Warfare–Related Dual Use Exports to Iraq and Their Possible Impact on the Health Consequences of the Persian Gulf War," published on May 25 and October 7, 1994.

The prewar fears about Iraqi chemical and biological capability are frequently cited in the autobiographies of the two key players. See *It Doesn't Take a Hero*, by Norman Schwarzkopf, with Peter Petre, published in 1992 by Bantam Books, and *My American Journey*, by Colin Powell, with Joseph E. Persico, published in 1995 by Random House. Rick Atkinson of the *Washington Post* deals with Iraqi germs and gases in *Crusade: The Untold Story of the Persian Gulf War*, published by Houghton Mifflin in 1993; so do Michael R. Gordon of the *New York Times* and retired Marine General Bernard E. Trainor in *The General's War: The Inside Story of the Conflict in the Gulf*, published by Little, Brown in 1995. For a darker view of the government's handling of the Khamisiyah bombing, see ex–CIA analyst Patrick G. Eddingston's account, *Gassed in the Gulf: The Inside Story of the Pentagon-CIA Cover-up of Gulf War Syndrome*, published in 1997 by Insignia Publishing Company of Washington. The cited essay by William M. Arkin is "The Gulf War and Its Syndrome," in the spring 1998 edition of *The Washington Quarterly* at page 53.

The most comprehensive information on Agent Orange and the long-running legal battles surrounding it can be obtained from the Agent Orange Resource Center, 2001 S St. NW, Washington, DC 20009. The best contact point for Gulf War veterans is the National Gulf War Resource Center, 1224 M St. NW, Washington, DC 20005. Swords to Plowshares, the veterans'-rights group that produced Dan Fahey's 1998 report on depleted uranium, is located at 995 Market St., San Francisco, CA 94103.

The cited newspaper stories on the effects of DU are "The Catastrophe Blair, Clinton and Saddam Have in Common," by Robert Fisk, the *London Independent*, page 17, March 9, 1998, and "Iraqi Cancers May Hold Clue to Gulf War Illness," by John Donnelly, *San Jose Mercury-News,* March 19, 1998, page 1. For an account of the media's inability to initially perceive the import of the Gulf War veterans' plight, see "Missed Story Syndrome: Why Did the National Media Ignore Gulf War Illness?" by Kate McKenna, in *AJR, the American Journalism Review*, May 1997, at page 22.

The Presidential Advisory Committee on Gulf War Veterans' Illnesses published a one-volume special report on its findings in October 1997 that is available from the committee at 1411 K St. NW, Suite 1000, Washington, DC 20005-3404. The Annual Report of the Pentagon's Office of the Special Assistant for Gulf War Illness, published in November 1997, is available on a special GulfLINK Web site on the Internet at www.gulflink.osd.mil. All of the military's special reports on the Gulf War, including a summary of its findings on the destruction of nerve gas at Khamisiyah, are posted on the site.

ABOUT THE AUTHOR

SEYMOUR M. HERSH is one of America's premier investigative reporters. In 1969, as a freelance journalist, he wrote the first account of the My Lai massacre in South Vietnam. In the 1970s, he worked at the *New York Times* in Washington and New York, and has rejoined the paper twice on special assignment. He has won more than a dozen major journalism prizes, including the 1970 Pulitzer Prize for International Reporting and four George Polk Awards. Hersh is the author of seven other books, including *The Price of Power: Kissinger in the Nixon White House*, which won the National Book Critics Circle Award and the *Los Angeles Times* Book Award, *The Target Is Destroyed: What Really Happened to Flight 007 and What America Knew About It*, *The Samson Option: Israel's Nuclear Arsenal and America's Foreign Policy*, and *The Dark Side of Camelot*. He lives in Washington, D.C., with his wife and three children.

A Note on The Library of Contemporary Thought

This exciting new monthly series tackles today's most provocative, fascinating, and relevant issues, giving top opinion makers a forum to explore topics that matter urgently to themselves and their readers. Some will be think pieces. Some will be research oriented. Some will be journalistic in nature. The form is wide open, but the aim is the same: to say things that need saying.

Look for these titles coming soon from
The Library of Contemporary Thought

EDWIN SCHLOSSBERG
INTERACTIVE EXCELLENCE
Defining and Developing New Standards for the
Twenty-first Century

ANNA QUINDLEN
HOW READING CHANGED MY LIFE